Cycling in South Wales

Rosemary Evans

Published by Sigma Leisure – an imprint of
Sigma Press, 1 South Oak Lane, Wilmslow, Cheshire SK9 6AR, England.

British Library Cataloguing in Publication Data
A CIP record for this book is available from the British Library.

ISBN: 1-85058-395-1

Typesetting and Design by: Sigma Press, Wilmslow, Cheshire.

Cover picture: Rosemary Evans on the Taff Trail, near Pontypridd (*photo: Martin Evans*)

Printed by: Manchester Free Press

Preface

Only a cyclist can write a guide book for cyclists!

That's so obvious, nobody seems to have thought of it. A guide book designed for motorists will tell you it's ten miles to the pub, but you need a cyclist to add that six of them are uphill, so you can assess your chances of making it before closing time.

The routes in this book are similar to rides I arranged for a Club which includes families with quite young children. Some runs are more strenuous than others, but none are unduly hard – otherwise I wouldn't be able to do them!

The super-fit and energetic cyclist can easily link one ride with the next to provide a greater challenge. It doesn't matter a bit whether you do 8 miles or 80, as long as you enjoy them all.

Most of the rides start from a point of interest, but this is a bonus. If the 'attraction', be it Castle, Museum, Nature Park or whatever, happens to be closed when you arrive, or it's simply not something which takes your fancy, you won't lose out. The ride's the thing.

I owe thanks to many people for their help in producing this book – my daughter Felicity for her research, my daughter Hilary for cheerfully slowing down to ride at my pace, my touring friends, Llantwit Major CTC, and at the last, the best – my husband Martin, who provided tea and sympathy, and placed his professional expertise with maps unstintingly at my disposal.

Rosemary Evans

CONTENTS

SOUTH WALES: custom-made for cyclists

THE RIDES

Appendix

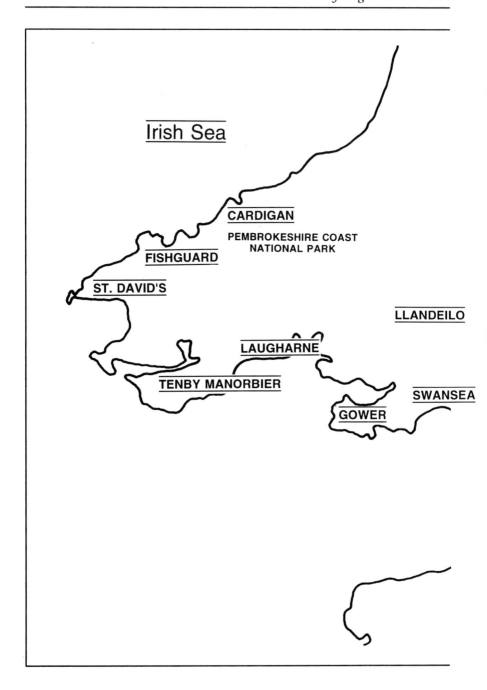

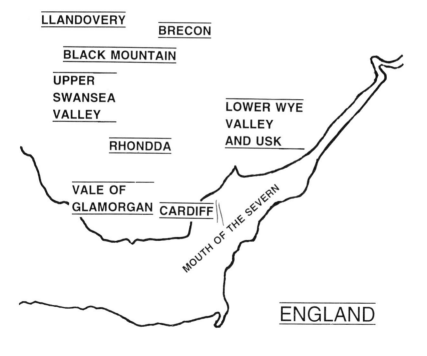

LLANDOVERY

BRECON

BLACK MOUNTAIN

UPPER
SWANSEA
VALLEY

LOWER WYE
VALLEY
AND USK

RHONDDA

VALE OF
GLAMORGAN CARDIFF

MOUTH OF THE SEVERN

ENGLAND

SOUTH WALES:
custom-made for cyclists

South Wales is a land of great variety, with adventure in easy-to-handle slices. It's remote enough to enjoy the peace of being 'in the middle of nowhere' while at the same time having the comfort of knowing that you're almost always within an hour's ride of a pub.

It's a hilly country, but not intimidatingly so. Remember that what goes up can have fun coming down! Select mountains and moorlands, or the scenic coastal rides, for exhilarating runs and dramatic views. In another mood, travel at an unhurried pace along wandering country lanes, or through wooded valleys with a gurgling stream for company.

The best months for a visit are March through to early July, or September and October. Spring brings the wild flowers and increasingly long evenings, when you can savour the pleasure of eating out of doors, before riding back without the bother of cycle lights. September and October are often fine and dry. The mixed woodlands and heather covered hills are particularly lovely in their autumn colours.

The school holiday months of July and August mean pressure on accommodation and, what's worse from a cyclist's point of view, a big increase in traffic in popular areas such as the Gower and the West Wales coastal resorts. Towed caravans, which get into difficulties on steep hills and narrow roads, can be a problem. Book accommodation ahead and start your rides early in the day if you can, during these periods.

Wales is well-known for its homely hospitality. Relax in small friendly 'locals' or the larger, ancient inns, where it's easy to imagine the clatter of stage-coaches on the cobbled yard. 'Pub grub' has improved enormously in recent years with much more emphasis on home-made food. The Wales Tourist Board promotes a scheme to encourage the use of traditional Welsh products. Participating eateries have a distinctive sign incorporating the Welsh Dragon and the words 'Blas ar Gymru'/Taste of Wales. They are also listed in 'Wales – Good Eating Guide', available from Tourist Information Centres and bookshops.

Welsh Wales: an introduction

A visitor's contact with the Welsh language comes through the place names. Everyone knows that a typical Welsh village is called Llan-something. 'Llan' is said to mean 'a church', but there's more to it than that.

Way back in the Bronze Age, two thousand years before Christ and the sign of the Cross, burials were symbolised by a circle. The dead were often cremated and the remains placed within a ring of stones. Chris Barber, in his book *More Mysterious Wales* considers it "quite possible that the word (Llan) reflects memories of worship held within stone circles."

Later, Christian churchyards were contained within walled enclosures, and 'Llan' signified the enclosed area, which could embrace not just a church with its churchyard, but also the monastery to which the church was attached – often a whole community.

Place names

Finding your way around Wales isn't made any easier when a place has both an English and a Welsh name, as Aberhonddu/Brecon, or Abertawe/Swansea. Also, the spelling of Welsh names varies. Two signposts pointing to the same village may use different interpretations of its name and your map could disagree with them both. Names based on Celtic Saints show the greatest diversity. Merthyr-Cynog, Llangynog and Defynnog all commemorate St Cynog. St Cadoc, or Cattwg, has a whole clutch of Llangattocks in his honour – Llangattock Lingoed, Llangattock-Vibon-Avel and Llangattock-nigh-Usk, as well as couple of Llangadogs and Cadoxtons.

Some Saints had a higher rating than others. One of the most popular, after St David, was St Teilo, with a score of dedications, including Llandeilo, Llantilio Crosseny, Llandeilo'r Fan and Llandeilo Llwydarth, on top of a one-third share in Llandaff Cathedral.

Names have a strange magic, a sacred identity of their own, which makes people fear to tamper with them. Their inhabitants may use English as their everyday language, but towns and villages have kept their Welsh names, to remind people of their inheritance. The names speak of flour mills and fulling mills, tanneries and dovecotes. 'Maes' and 'Coed' in street names are often all that's left of the meadows and woods buried beneath the houses.

Knowing a few of the commonest elements of Welsh names can turn even the most daunting collection of letters into something meaningful. Many names give a full topographical description all tied up in one word, like 'Penyrheolgerrig'. That would look quite a mouthful in English too, if you were to write 'thevillageatthetopofthestonyroad' in one go.

'Aber' means the mouth of a river, and is usually followed by the river's name, as in Aberdare, Aberthaw, Aberdeen. Spot the one with an identity problem.

Descriptive elements are built up and shifted around. *Cefn*, a ridge, exists on its own, and combines with *Coed*, a wood, or with *Craig*, a rocky place, to form *Cefn Coed* and *Cefn Craig*. Sometimes two elements aren't enough, so we have *Cefn Coed y Cymer* – 'The ridge with a wood at the joining of the rivers'.

The commonest physical features, rivers, hills, and woods, combine with one another or with landmarks such as a mill. Most villages had a flour mill, Y Felin, so it's necessary to add Felin-fach, the small mill, Felin-ganol, the middle mill, or Felin Newydd, the new mill, and so on. (Strictly speaking, 'mill' translates as 'melin', but Welsh initial letters play musical chairs. This happens mostly to feminine nouns and makes looking up words in a dictionary difficult for non-Welsh speakers.) Valleys, whether *Cwm*, a coombe or wooded valley, *Ystrad*, a wide valley, or *Pant*, a hollow or valley, imply a stream, so there would be a *Pont* (bridge) or a *Rhyd* (Ford), or both, as in Pontyrhyd.

You can have fun inventing authentic sounding Welsh names. Some might turn out to exist – Pant-y-Pont could be a possibility. Pant-y-Hose might not be.

Get by in Welsh!

Finally – ten Welsh words it may pay to recognise, though you'll soon find out if you get them wrong.

Beicio	–	to cycle
Beiciau	–	bicycles
Dim	–	no; so *'Dim beiciau'* means No Cycling.
Perygl	–	danger.
Dynion	–	the Gents
Merched	–	the Ladies
Ar agor	–	open; as, hopefully, on pub doors.
Ar gau	–	closed.
Diolch yn Fawr	–	thanks very much
Hwyl Fawr	–	the best of luck.

And the real essential that everyone knows – *iechyd da!* (literally, 'Good Health'). This is the only one you actually need to know how to say. If you're English speaking, something roughly like 'yacky dah' will do, as long as you buy the drinks!

Lots of books offer a guide to Welsh pronunciation. Try by all means, but the strange choking sounds you produce won't fool a Welsh speaker for one moment. I've lived in Wales for 35 years but a couple I asked for directions recently couldn't resist smiling at the way I pronounced the place name. 'You shouldn't be laughing, she's English, mind', the wife chided her husband. 'And we know where it is she means'.

Safety note

Cycling on the highway is a potentially dangerous activity. Children must be supervised and all cyclists must carefully observe the Highway Code. Neither the author nor the publisher can be held responsible for the condition of any route described in this book; you follow such routes at your own risk.

Having said that, I hope you enjoy the rides and will come back again for many years.

Hwyl fawr and *Happy Cycling.*

Overleaf: The Severn Bridge (Wales Tourist Board)

1. Croeso y Gymru!

Over the first Severn Bridge to Chepstow, Gwent.

Distance: 5.5mls/9km

Longer Options: Rides 1 to 4 combine to make a full day out for stronger riders. With a short linking ride to Monmouth, they form the start of a South Wales Tour. Taken separately, they make bite-sized rides for people who prefer an easier pace, with leisure for sightseeing.

Terrain: The Severn Bridge is the flattest bit of Wales!

Accommodation/Refreshments/Supplies: Severn View Pavilion motorway services are cycle friendly. Ride up to picnic area by the Coach park for easy access to snacks, shop, toilets. Chepstow is well provided with hotels, guest houses, B&Bs, pubs, cafés and shops. The Castle View Hotel (facing Castle car park), welcomes cyclists and offers a 5% discount on production of this book. Tel: (0291) 620349.

Toilets: Castle Car Park. Riverside.

Rail Access: Chepstow links with Bristol/Cheltenham, and Newport/Cardiff. Bristol Parkway (Intercity) is 8mls/13km SE. Severn Beach 5mls/8km south on the English side. Severn Tunnel Junction on Welsh side.

Tourist Information: In Castle Car Park.

Things to see on this Ride: River Severn. Chepstow, Historic border-fortress town, with twisty streets, Castle, Museum, Medieval Walls and Town Gate.

Next Rides: Lower Wye Valley Rides. Ride 2 Chepstow to Tintern. Ride 3 Tintern to Trellech. Ride 4 Trellech to Penallt Old Church.

Route

The Severn Bridge Cycle track is on the North or upstream side of the bridge. The bridge itself is shown in the picture facing this page. The start is signposted from the access road leading up to Severn View Pavilion services.

If you have ridden from Bristol, where Sigma Leisure's 'Cycling in the Cotswolds' finishes, there is a sign on the A403 Avonmouth road, indicating that the Cycle Track is straight ahead at the roundabout on junction 21 of the M4. Follow the signs to the Services. Keep going up the hill for a hundred yards or so until you see another sign to the Cycle Track on your left. Don't turn off the roundabout too early or you'll be the wrong side of the barrier.

The Cycle Track is used by cyclists in both directions and also by Works vehicles. Pedestrians have their own path on the opposite side of the bridge. There's a speed limit of 15 mph (24km), but it's breezy up here. If there's a head-wind you won't find it hard to keep within it. In very blustery weather, bicycles and high vehicles are not allowed to cross.

It's an exhilarating ride. There's a sense of voyaging to another land as you watch the cables sway and the current swirl. You ride high above the 'Severn strong, rolling on rough waters brown, white aspen leaves along'. The tide rises and falls as much as 53 feet (16 metres). Make a return crossing even a short while later, and the river-scape will have changed. Travelling from east to west, you're riding counter to the traffic. Stop and put your feet down to feel the trampoline effect as heavy vehicles pound by.

Before the bridge was built in 1966, there were two recognised Severn ferry crossings, the Old Passage from Aust to Beachley, and the New Passage, three miles further downstream. The Old Passage passes diagonally under the bridge and was used by the car ferry. A ramp on the Aust side and the abandoned jetty at Beachley can still be seen.

The New Passage was a crossing place since the earliest times. During the Civil War (1642-9), boatmen with Royalist sympathies drowned fifty or sixty of Cromwell's troops by leaving them stranded on the rocks called the English Stones. Stage coaches carrying the Royal Mail between London and Milford used the New Passage from 1785 until 1826. Now, the second Severn bridge is under construction here. (Due to open early 1996).

The Beachley peninsula separates the mouth of the Wye from the Severn. It's taken up almost entirely with the Army Apprentices' College. Motorists must pay for the privilege of entering Wales, but cyclists cross free. At the end of the track there's a sign 'Cyclists Dismount' and a barrier. Negotiate the edge of the Thornwell roundabout to pick up start of Chepstow Cycle Path. Ride beside the A466, climbing gently for one mile, to the roundabout at High Beech. Turn right into Newport Road for Chepstow.

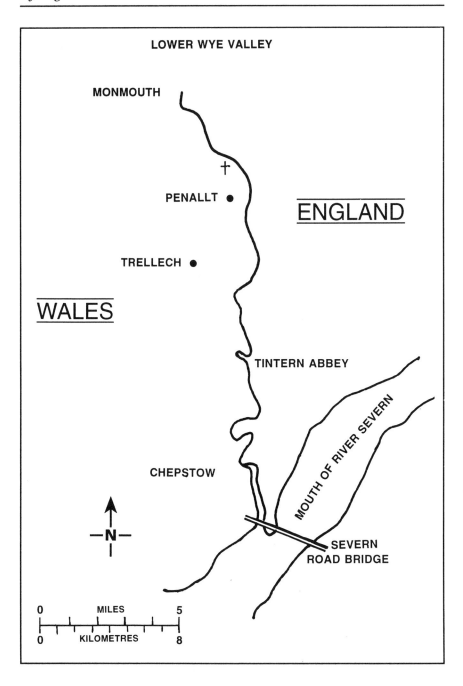

Chepstow/Casgwent

The original English name was probably 'Cheap Stow,' meaning 'a market place'. The Normans built Chepstow Castle soon after the Conquest, (1066 and all that). Grandly poised on the 'steep and lofty' crags above the swiftly flowing Wye, it's one of the earliest stone-built castles in Britain. It was improved several times between the 12th and 17th centuries, until, like so many other Castles in South Wales, it became 'one of the ruins which Cromwell knocked about a bit' in the Civil War. An exhibition at the site, 'A Castle at War' illustrates a battle scene with life-size models.

Much of the 13th century Port Wall which surrounded the medieval town on its landward sides still remains. The 13th century Town Gate, through which modern traffic squeezes, was once the only road into town. It had a major restoration in 1524.

Chepstow is 'twinned' with the town of Cormeilles in Normandy, France, where the builder of Chepstow Castle also founded a Benedictine priory.

2. Wordsworth's 'Sylvan Wye'

Chepstow – Tintern – Chepstow

Distance: 12.5mls/20km.

Longer Options: Continue with next rides: Ride 3, Tintern to Trellech = 12.5mls/ 20km; Ride 4, Trellech to Penallt Old Church = 13 mls/21km; Ride 5, Continue to Monmouth. Rides 6 and 7 start in Usk.

Terrain: Moderately hilly. Climbs to 755ft/230m.

Accommodation/Refreshments/Supplies: Chepstow as described for Ride 1. Hotels, pubs and teashops in Tintern/Tintern Parva.

Toilets: Chepstow Castle car park. Tintern Abbey. Tintern and Tintern Old Station.

Rail Access: Chepstow connects with Bristol/Cheltenham/Gloucester and Cardiff/ Newport. See also Page 4.

Tourist Information: Chepstow Castle car park. Tintern Abbey, Tintern Old Station.

Things to see on this Ride: Between them, this ride and Rides 3 and 4 cover most of the historic and beautiful Lower Wye Valley. Superb river and woodland scenery. Chepstow, as described in Ride 1. Tintern Abbey and Abbey Mill.

How to Connect with Next Rides: Ride 3 begins in Tintern. Rides 4 and 5 continue from Ride 3. A most enjoyable ride to Usk for Rides 6 and 7 is as follows: Go ahead to Devauden instead of turning left to The Cot. From Devauden, take the B4293, signed Itton, but immediately turn right after leaving the Green, on very minor road to Wolvesnewton and Langwm.

Route

Starting Point: Chepstow Castle.

Leave the square and turn left, downhill and One-Way. The Museum is opposite. At traffic lights in front of bridge, filter right. A few yards down the next turning on the left brings you to the river bank, from where in 1840, the leaders of a Chartists' revolt were transported to Tasmania. All the workers' rights they demanded have since been

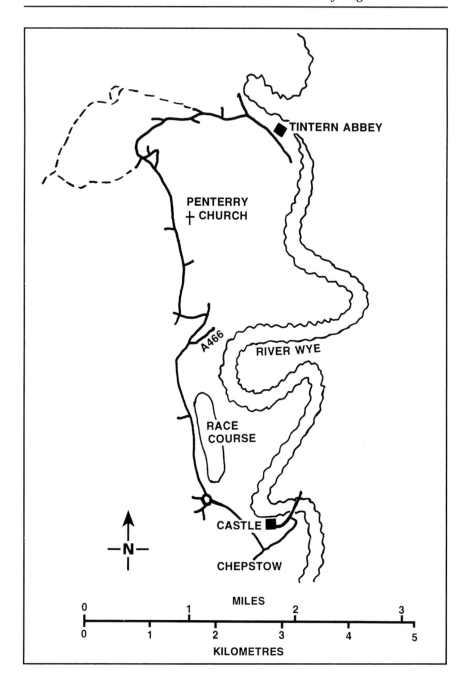

granted, except one – their request for Annual General Elections. The Wye is very fast flowing but brown and muddy, especially at low tide.

Return to the road, which turns right, then zigzags right and left, through Lower Church Street into Church Road. St Mary's Church, formerly part of a Benedictine Abbey, contemporary with the Castle, is on your left.

Follow signs to Town Centre at junction, (Nelson Street) and turn right with care into Station Road – traffic joins here from the opposite direction. At traffic lights, turn left into Beaufort Square and continue up the shopping street to the Town Gate. Traffic lights on the hill are awkward. Go through the Gate and immediately turn right into Welsh Street.

Chepstow Castle (Wales Tourist Board)

A last glimpse of the Castle down to your right, and a steady pull up out of Chepstow for a mile and a bit, before a dip down to the St Lawrence roundabout.

Turn right onto the A466 and ride alongside Chepstow race-course. No free view of the races, though, it's enclosed by a high stone wall. On

Sundays beware of cars jostling to get into vast outdoor market on the left. Ride for 1.5 miles, pass name-sign for St Arvans, ride uphill one mile.

Where the A466 makes a right-angled turn to the right, keep straight ahead into a minor road signed 'Wyndcliffe'. Pass Forestry Commission car park on your right, as road bends left. (A footpath from here leads to 'The Eagle's Nest', a viewpoint 700ft/213m above the river).

Ride half a mile uphill and turn right at crossroads with Wyndcliffe Court. Continue a non-violent climb. Within a mile, a gate on your right indicates the path to Penterry Church, its bell and Cross just visible, as it sits marooned in muddy fields, with no road access at all.

Ride along the ridge, then descend through woods of beech and oak, thick enough to block most of the light. After half a mile come briefly into the open at a crossroads, with unmade track on the right. Go straight on, following sign to Tintern.

The ground is generally wet and slippery with old leaves and debris from the trees. As you turn the corner past the farm, it's even more slippery, though not with droppings from the trees! Wind downhill through the woods for another mile. Pass the back of the tiny Cherry Tree pub (Real Ale, draught Cider), and turn right at junction. Continue down, to reach the A466 beside the Royal George Hotel. Tintern Abbey can be seen down the road to your right. The Abbey Mill is a few yards to your left.

To return to Chepstow, go back to the Royal George Hotel and the road you came in by, which is signed Llanishen. Keep to the right at first junction, signed Devauden, to pass the front of the Cherry Tree, with its guardian stream. The road follows the lively stream up a gentle valley, a delightful ride. After 1.5 miles, pass a tidied-up Ancient Iron Mine on your right. In another half mile, you come to a bridge on your right where the river is dammed to make a deep pool for angling. Sit quietly to see the fish. Don't cross here, keep straight on, following sign to Devauden. Cross river by next bridge in a quarter of a mile, and turn left uphill. It's a barely perceptible slope for a mile beside the stream, which is forced to squeeze through a couple of dams in artificial waterfalls. Then you leave the water and begin a more positive climb for half a mile. Only your panting can be heard in the deep stillness of the woods. (Continue straight ahead here to go to Usk).

Take a left turn signed The Cot and ride past a cluster of cottages. Downhill to a stream, and up the other side.

Right at a T-junction signed St Arvans. You should recognise the road as the one you rode earlier, in the opposite direction. This way it's uphill to start, then a run down, with a clear view of Chepstow race-course, to the crossroads at Wyndcliffe Court. From here you retrace your wheel marks to Chepstow.

Tintern

Tintern Abbey is a Cistercian monastic ruin, of haunting beauty. Founded in 1131 AD, it was one of the casualties of Henry VIII's Dissolution of the Monasteries, in 1536. The buildings there now cover a time span of 400 years. You'll find guided tours, information, and a shop here.

The Abbey Mill, a quarter of a mile up the Monmouth road, is contemporary with the Abbey. Trout from the Mill ponds feature on the café menu. Craft shop.

Tintern Old Station is half a mile along the road in the Monmouth direction. Snuggled in between road and river, the railway station 'axed' a generation ago is now a picnic area, with carriages turned into an Information centre, and in summer, a café. Signals and station equipment are still in place.

3. 'Steep and Lofty Cliffs'

Tintern – Trellech – Tintern

Distance: 12.5mls/20km. (Back to Chepstow, 20mls/ 32km).

Longer Options: Continue to Penallt, Ride 4, 13mls/21km. Continue to Monmouth for Ride 5 or to Usk for Rides 6 and 7.

Shorter Options: Returning to Chepstow on the B4293 is flatter and would save a few miles. It's a pleasant if less exciting road and not usually too busy.

Terrain: Some hills, but nothing fearsome.

Accommodation/Refreshments/Supplies: Tintern as described for Ride 2. Pubs and village shops in Trellech.

Toilets: Tintern Abbey. Tintern. Tintern Old Station. Whitestone picnic site.

Rail Access: Chepstow.

Tourist Information: Tintern Abbey. Tintern Old Station.

Things to see on this Ride: Tintern, as described in Ride 2. Trellech. Harold's Stones. The Virtuous Well. Terret Tump. Medieval Preaching Cross and 13th century church. The Lion Real Ale pub. 'The house-less woods, the landscape with the quiet of the sky' and 'sportive wood run wild' as Wordsworth has it.

How to Connect with Next Rides: Ride 4 begins in Trellech. Ride 5, continue to Monmouth from Ride 4. Rides 6 & 7 start in Usk. To reach Usk from Trellech, take the B4293 to just south of Llanishen. Turn right and go down Star Hill. Views of Sugar Loaf and Black Mountains. The 400 year old Star Inn is worth stopping for. Go through Llansoy to the B4235 which goes to Usk.

Route

Starting Point: Tintern Abbey.

Turn on to the A466 in direction of Monmouth. Ride beside the river, past the Abbey Mill. Toilets are on your right a bit further on. In another quarter mile, as you come round a bend into Tintern Parva, turn left, signed to Catbrook. The Wye Valley Hotel is on the corner. A steady climb for a mile and a half on this minor but wider than usual road.

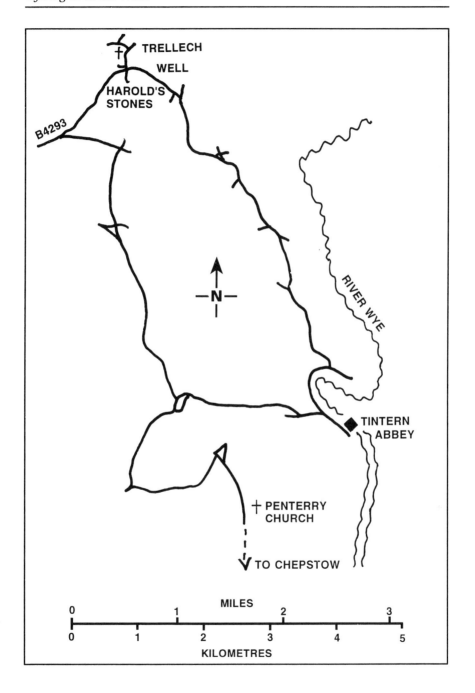

Pass a sign to 'Botany Bay' on your left. An odd name for a place so far inland, it appears that prisoners were collected here before being despatched to Bristol for transportation. Turn left at a T-junction, opposite the Forestry Commission picnic site 'Whitestone'. There are toilets here.

A moderately steep climb, past Ninewells Wood parking spot, then ride two and a half miles to Trellech. As you pass the place-name sign on your approach to Trellech, only a few yards from the road, the Virtuous Well can be seen in a meadow to your right.

Turn right at the junction and immediately right again. Before going up the hill, look for a large display board on your left, which lists interesting sights in the vicinity. The Board is on the corner of the drive leading to Court Farm. Follow this for a couple of hundred yards towards the farmhouse, and you come to Tump Terret, a Castle Mound dating back to the thirteenth century. It still has a (dry) moat surrounding it.

At the top of the hill, Trellech Church, dating from the 14th century, is worth a visit. There are instructions pinned to the door telling you where to ask for the key if it's locked.

The vicar has a kindlier style than many, whose Notices in porches often sound peremptory. Speaking of stiletto heels, this one avoids comment except to say that there is a grille in the centre aisle. The Post office, just round the corner from the church, has an interesting slit window. The Lion, a 17th Century pub, Free House, Real Ale, is opposite the church. Lower down the hill is The Village Green Inn, next to the Village Stores.

Leaving Trellech, ride to the bottom of the hill towards Chepstow and stick to the B4293 when it swerves right. Harold's Stones are in a field on the left, with a gate to the road, after 200 yards.

Go on for a mile, and take first turn left, with a sign to Parkhouse Tavern. Turn right at crossroads. A lazy mile and the friendly local pub, smothered in Virginia creeper, is on your right. A further downhill mile brings you to The Fountain, a popular whitewashed Inn, originally 17th century but modernised. Carry on down, through a deeply wooded valley, with a stream dodging from one side of the road to the other. A good road for a whizz but a shame to miss the scenery. At the bottom, the road abruptly turns left across a bridge, signed to Tintern. Go this way if you wish to return to Tintern. Continue by the stream, past

Ancient Iron Works on your left, and the Cherry Tree Pub on your right. You will arrive beside the Royal George Hotel in Tintern.

To return to Chepstow: don't cross the bridge, but bear right into minor road, round by Lilac Cottage. Pass another stone bridge on your left in a quarter of a mile, and begin gradual climb beside river, past a couple of dams, and a steeper half mile to The Cot turning on your left. Then continue with instructions in previous ride.

Tintern

Tintern is described in Ride 2.

Tintern Abbey (Wales Tourist Board)

Trellech

Trellech was a settlement in prehistoric times. Its name means Three Stones, and the three Standing Stones known as Harold's Stones are Bronze Age or earlier (see next ride for a picture). No-one is sure of their purpose, but some astrological significance seems likely. The Roman road from Monmouth to Chepstow came through here. The Church of St Nicholas is over 600 years old. The Preaching Cross in the churchyard is over 1,000 years old, and so is the strangely-fashioned stone structure nearby. Nobody knows for certain what this is. It's thought to be a Druidic altar.

The Virtuous Well, or St Anne's Well, contains several springs. Each was believed to have the power to cure a different malady. The waters are rich in iron, so may indeed have been beneficial for some ailments. It's a very pretty little stone well, with niches for drinking vessels. People still place fresh flowers there.

By the 13th century, Trellech was a flourishing centre of real importance. It was destroyed by local enemies in 1291. Barely recovered, the Black Death overcame the town in the mid-1300s, and it was reduced to 'a poore inconsiderable village' by Owain Glyndŵr in the early 1400s.

4. A wander through the woods

Trellech – Penallt Old Church – Trellech

Distance: 13mls/21km

Longer Options: Continue to Monmouth (4mls/6.4km) and join Ride 5 to Raglan, 29mls/47km. Connect with Rides 6 or 7 at Usk (20mls/32km and 8mls/13km).

Terrain: Definitely hilly.

Accommodation/Refreshments/Supplies: Accommodation in Monmouth as described for Ride 5. Trellech as given in Ride 3. The Trekkers at Narth. The Bush at Pentwyn. The Boat in Penallt.

Toilets: Plenty of cover in the woods.

Rail Access: Chepstow 14mls/22.5km South, or Abergavenny 14mls/22.5km West.

Things to see on this Ride: Woodland and river scenery. Penallt Old Church. The pubs – a feast of Real Ales, and cosy and welcoming with lots to offer those who don't want alcohol.

How to Connect with Next Rides: Ride 5 starts in Monmouth, 4mls/6.4km from Penallt. Rides 6 & 7 begin in Usk. Directions to Usk in previous ride.

Route

Take the road which curves past The Lion, signposted to Maryland and The Narth. A short rise, then ride through very pretty woodland, mainly beech trees, but larches, oaks, and horse chestnuts amongst them. The occasional maple and a bit of holly in there too. The road winds all over the place. Pass The Trekkers pub on your right. After 2.5 miles, straight ahead at crossroads. In a mile, cross a common where the Kiln Tump plaque commemorates the use of the land as common land since 1581. Straight on at the crossroads, into Penallt, sometimes shown as Pentwyn on maps. Pass St Mary's (New Church), and the Vicarage. (The Vicar's also responsible for Old Church. Services held there on the first and third Sunday each month).

Set back from the road is The Bush pub, large but snug with valley views from its terrace (Bass and HB on offer). Just past The Bush, turn left.

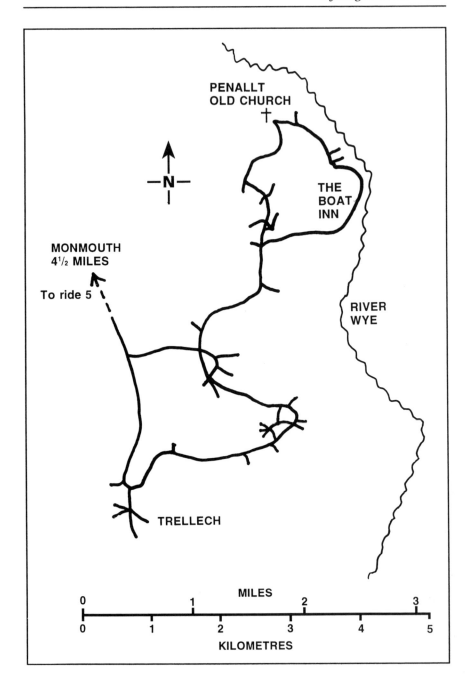

Plunge sharply downhill, but not too fast at first as you have to turn right in a few hundred yards. Now there's a straight downhill ahead of you, through woods, until you shoot up in front of the church.

Penallt Old Church perches on a pinnacle, draped in woods, and surveys the valley, far from all disturbance. Although much restored, parts of the church are believed to date from the 1200s.

On down a narrow corridor of overhanging woods, hemmed in by high stone walls. Too mossy and slippy to take full advantage of the gradient – it's wet most of the year. The road's rarely used – but a postbox on a wall suggests you might meet a GPO van sometime. The roadway has 7 feet 3 inches/2.2m of hard surface. A bicycle (mine, anyway!) needs half that to feel comfortable, so even another cyclist head-on makes for a crowd.

After three quarters of a mile, just past 'The Birches' there are a couple of vicious hairpins which will have all but the biggest Tarzans running out of bottom gears. Never mind if you're brought to your feet, it's only a yard or two till you reach The Boat pub, close beside the river Wye, offering an array of Real Ales, guest beers and home-made curries.

The name is not altogether fanciful – floods some years ago made getting there by boat the only option.

The chief stone of "Harold's Stones", Trellech

But it's not as remote as it seems to the hardy souls who get there the pretty way. The old railway bridge connects with Redbrook and the A466 across the river, allowing crowds to arrive on summer evenings and weekends.

From The Boat it's a mile and a quarter uphill to the top of Lone Lane. (If you wish to continue to Monmouth, go straight ahead here and it's downhill all the way.)

Turn left and ride one mile back to crossroads where you were earlier. Turn right. In half a mile turn left on the B4293 to return to Trellech.

5. Lost Battles

Monmouth – White Castle – Llantilio Crossenny – Raglan Castle – Monmouth.

Distance: 29mls/47km.

Longer Option: Continue to Usk for Rides 6 and 7.

Shorter Option: Omitting White Castle reduces ride by 3 miles, and avoids a hill. Riding to Raglan after passing Parc Grace-Dieu would total 22mls/34km. Go through Raglan town to roundabout to west of castle.

Terrain: Rolling country throughout, nothing too severe but few totally flat bits.

Accommodation/Refreshments/supplies: Good range of Hotels, Guest Houses, pubs, cafés, shops and chain-stores in Monmouth. Youth Hostel(once part of a 15th century Priory) in Priory Street, Monmouth. Talocher Farmhouse Hotel at Wonastow (beside route, good views); tel: 0600 83662. Beaufort Arms Hotel in Raglan. Camping site at Dingestow. Hostry Inn, 15th century village pub, Real Ale, in Llantilio Crossenny.

Toilets: In car park near Monnow Bridge. At Raglan Castle.

Tourist Information: Shire Hall, Monmouth; tel: 0600 713899 (summer)

Rail Access: Nearest Station Abergavenny, 12mls/20km.

Things to see on this Ride: Monmouth – Castle ruins, Monnow fortified bridge, Nelson Museum, Coaching Inns. Rich pastoral scenery. Real Ale pub. Raglan Castle, medieval masonry. White Castle – optional diversion – another medieval hilltop Castle. Livestock market Mondays and Fridays.

How to Connect with Next Rides: Ride 6 is centred on Usk. Ride 7, Caerleon – Usk – Caerleon. Go back to roundabout before Raglan Castle and take minor road (the Old Raglan Road) signed to Usk via Gwehlog. Pass The Hall, small pub, features in Good Beer Guide. Raglan to Usk is 5.5mls/9km.

Route

Leave Monmouth by the Monnow bridge. Go right at roundabout and in 200 yards, turn left into minor road, signed Wonastow/Dingstow. Pass strikingly placed War Memorial to your left, on bend at top of hill. In 2 miles take right turn uphill to Hendre. The road coils its way into the hills, down and up, round and about, for 3 miles, passing a few farms but nothing else. Offa's Dyke Long Distance path meets the road, just before a sharp descent. Unfortunately, bends prevent your keeping up your speed ready for the next rise. Half a mile from Hendre, and almost opposite a golf course, turn left, signed Tregare/Raglan. Down to a stream and up the other side, pass Parc Grace-Dieu farm, and take right turn by a grassy triangle into small road. (Keep straight on to shorten ride by going directly to Raglan). Pass modern bungalow and farm on your left, and immediately take steep right turn up through woods of beech and hawthorn. A short climb and then a sharp descent, with a couple of hairpins, down to the River Trothy. On your left is the quaint little church of St Michael's Llanvihangel Ystern Llewern – a grandiose name for somewhere that's not even a village, merely a parish. Still playing touch-and-go with Offa's Dyke path, turn right at junction, cross the river and ride uphill to Onen. Go left on the B4233, signed Abergavenny.

A mile or so ahead, a weathered old stone horse trough on the left is a reminder of the usual form of transport round here until quite recent times.

Just coming into Llantilio Crossenny there is a right turn leading up to White Castle. This military Norman Castle, first built in 1180, is more complete than many Castles, as it was never attacked. It occupies a wind-blown and attractively rural site on the top of quite a severe hill. If you need to fill your water bottles after the climb, there is a tap up here, but it's past the point at which you must pay for admission.

Back to the main road, take turning almost opposite for Llantilio Crossenny. If you didn't go up to the Castle, then this turning will be on your left. Left again in a quarter of a mile if you want to see the church. The Vicarage, where you may obtain the key, is the first house a little way further on, on the right.

The Hostry is a large whitewashed pub, popular with local cyclists on Sunday runs. The route turns left just before the Hostry. Cross a hump-backed bridge over the Trothy. Keep left when road divides, signed Penrhos. Left at junction, then in 100 yards, right. (Almost a crossroads). Keep right at junction for Penrhos. Left at Buddhist Centre into wooded lane with no sign. Pass Penrhos church on your left. Left at a T-junction with sign telling you where you were but not where you're

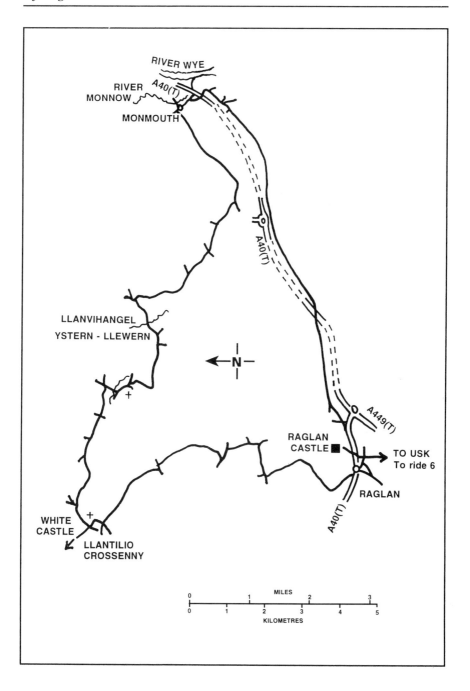

going. A flat bit of road with high hedges and poor visibility. Make towards Tregare church with its jolly weathercock, but turn right without passing it. Turn left for Raglan at next crossroads.

After a left bend, there's an excellent view of Raglan Castle a couple of fields away to your left, and of mountains to your right. At the T-junction turn left, (Give Way). At roundabout go left onto the A40 for about 400 yards. Access road for Raglan Castle is on your left.

Leaving the Castle, it's barely half a mile on the major road to a roundabout/junction, when you keep well over to the left for Mitchell Troy. This road follows the line of the A40, passing under it and then running parallel. When it seems as though you're fated to be drawn back into the traffic, the road makes a nifty right turn and continues alongside the A40, a hedgerow away. Follow road towards Monmouth Town Centre, turning right at roundabout to return across Monnow bridge.

Raglan Castle (Wales Tourist Board)

Monmouth

Monmouth is a tug-of-love town, claimed by both Welsh and English as their own. In the Civil War it was occupied by first one side and then the other. Once firmly, if a trifle anomalously, known as an English County, signs used to proclaim 'Welcome to Wales and Monmouthshire'. Today it's sure of its identity as a Gwent market town, with the imposing Shire Hall, built 1724, a reminder of times past. England-and-Wales go together like husband-and-wife. It was an arranged marriage, enforced in 1536 by Henry VIII, whose own unions had a poor track record, but after the best part of five hundred years, the pair have almost settled down.

Henry V was born in Monmouth. His most famous victory is celebrated in the name of Agincourt Square, the town's focal point. C.S. Rolls, forever linked with Royce, was another local man. Monmouth Castle has little left of it, but the Monnow Bridge, a fortified medieval bridge built in 1272, survives as the last of its kind in Britain. Monmouth was a staging point for the London to Milford mail coaches, and the Beaufort Arms established a good reputation for comfort and service. Wordsworth stayed there, and so did Admiral Nelson. The Nelson Museum in Priory Street has a grand display of Nelson's letters and weapons and even his glass eye! (Museum open daily all year, 10.00 to 1.00 pm, 2.00 to 5.00 pm, Sundays 2.00 – 5.00 pm)

Raglan Castle

With Castles in almost everyone's back yard in Wales, there are many claims to be the most impressive, or the most unusual. Raglan can put in a good bid with its four-storey gate-house, hexagonal towers and sweeping approach across the 16th century bridge. Raglan Castle is in the care of CADW, Welsh Historic Monuments. It's open daily.

6. A Riverside Ramble

Usk – Llantrisent – Newbridge-on-Usk – Tredunnoc – Llangybi – Usk

Distance: 10.5mls/17km.

Longer Option: Ride 6 is a short family ride. Through tourists and stronger riders may prefer Ride 7.

Terrain: Easy.

Accommodation/Refreshments/Supplies: Several small Hotels and a number of Pubs offer accommodation in Usk. The Gwent Tertiary College has cheap student-style accommodation and camping facilities during College vacations. B & B at The Greyhound, Llantrisent. Cwrt Bleddyn Hotel, Tredunnoc, 4-star. Pubs with good pub food are plentiful in the town, and there's a high density of excellent pubs on the ride. All necessary shops.

Toilets: In Maryport Street North car park in Usk.

Rail Access: Nearest station is Newport, Gwent; 16mls/26km. If you're travelling by train, it would be better to use Ride 7, Caerleon – Usk – Caerleon which starts 4mls/6.5km from Newport.

Tourist Information: Vale of Usk Tourist Association; Tel: 0291 672840. Display boards in Usk. Selection of books and leaflets at Gwent Rural Life Museum.

Things to see on this Ride: Usk – Roman town. River scenery. Choice of pubs.

How to Connect with Next Rides: Ride 7 is more strenuous than Ride 6. To use Ride 6 to reach Caerleon, turn left opposite Cwrt Bleddyn Hotel. To connect with Cardiff, see instructions in Ride 7.

Route

Starting Point: Clock tower in Market Square, Usk.

Take Priory Street, signed Llantrisent, from far right-hand corner. Ride round past St Mary's Priory church. Follow road round to your left, and pass H.M. Prison on your left as you come to the edge of town.

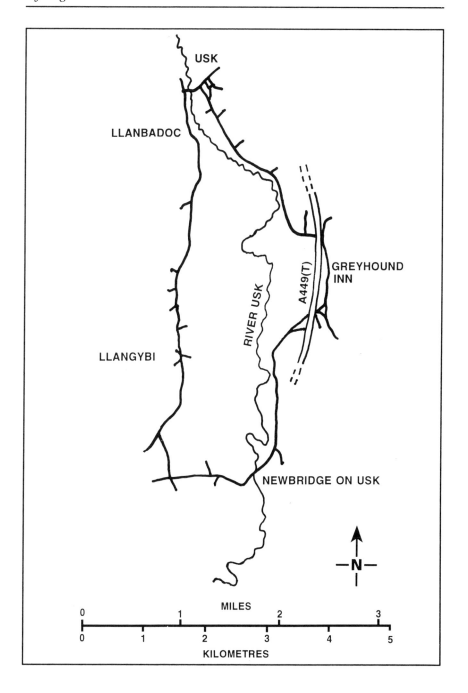

Ride a very flat mile to a little stream, and another mile imperceptibly downhill to another stream, at Llanllowell (Yes, it really does have three sets of 'll's)!

Pass a church on your right as the Usk Flood Route joins from your left, and go underneath the A449. There is a sign to the Usk Grass Ski Centre on your left. In under a mile you reach The Greyhound, a traditional country pub, almost certainly with a stack of bicycles outside on a summer Sunday. In half a mile, turn right at grass triangle, steeply down, signed Caerleon, and pass under the A449 again.

Ride parallel to main road on left and river on right. Turn right after 1 mile for Tredunnoc. Cross river, looking very much a classic salmon river at this point. The beautifully situated Newbridge Inn is on your right. Ride up a short hill – the only one on the ride, and not even a 'pipe-opener'. Turn right at crossroads signed Llangybi. Turn right on main road opposite Cwrt Bleddyn Hotel. The White Hart, a traditional coaching inn with two vast fireplaces to ensure a warm welcome, is on your right. Two easy miles back to Usk.

The square at Usk (Wales Tourist Board)

Usk

The name Usk derives from a Celtic word, Wsyg, meaning Water. Wsyg is also said to be the source word of Whisky, which perhaps says something about the Celts.

The Romans were in Usk even before they were in Caerleon. The XXth Legion was based here and took part in the defeat of Queen Boudicca or Boadicea in 61 AD. (She's the one with the scythes fastened to her chariot wheels, who has a monument at Westminster).

The Romans eventually withdrew, and in due course the Normans came, and built one of their Castles. This one was badly mauled in the Glyndŵr rebellion of 1403 and is very much a ruin. It's privately owned. After such a blood thirsty history, Usk is a pretty and peaceful riverside town, with many cobblestone pavements, antique shops for browsing, and the Gwent Rural Life Museum, open April until end October.

7. Roamin' with the Romans

Caerleon – Llandegfedd Reservoir – Usk – Caerleon.

Distance: 20mls/32km.

Longer Option: Continue to Cardiff for Ride 8.

Shorter Options: Going to Llangybi from the reservoir, (not visiting Usk) would reduce distance to 16mls/26km. Going direct to Caerleon instead of via Llanhennock saves little mileage but more energy.

Terrain: Undulating. One fierce (1:8) hill up from Sôr Brook.

Accommodation/Refreshments/Supplies: In Usk as described in Ride 6. Small hotels in Caerleon, several pubs and shops. Kiosk at Llandegfedd Reservoir.

Toilets: In car park by Ampitheatre in Caerleon. At Llandegfedd. In car park in Usk.

Rail Access: Newport. 4mls/6.4km from Caerleon. 90 minutes to London, direct routes to Midlands/The North/West Country.

Tourist Information: Office in Caerleon is in an imaginatively laid out courtyard, filled with craft shops, halfway up High Street. (High Street is One-Way uphill, anti-clockwise). Information boards at Llandegfedd. Leaflets in Gwent Rural Life Museum in Usk.

Things to see on this Ride: Caerleon – the Roman town of *Isca* – Ampitheatre, Roman Barracks, Roman Baths, Museum. Llandegfedd Reservoir – wildlife, water-sports. One of the most intensively used reservoirs in Britain. Usk – Roman town, described in Ride 6.

How to Connect with Next Rides: From Caerleon ride 4mls/6.4km to Newport on B4596. Cross river, join A48 heading for Cardiff. At 'Ebbw Bridge' roundabout before Junction 28 of M4, turn left onto B4239, signed St. Brides/Tredegar House. Ride over the Wentlooge Levels, known to local cyclists as the Newport Flats. You'll feel the wind from the 'sea' or mud flats half a mile away. Developments of one kind and another threaten this area but at the moment it's a lovely ride beside 'Rhines' or ditches, where herons and moorhens, mallards and dabchicks live. Horses, goats and cattle wander beside the road. There are three villages and four pubs, including the Six Bells at Peterstone, between Newport and Cardiff.

Route

Starting Point: The Roman Ampitheatre, Caerleon.

Turn left at end of road (one way). Ride alongside Green, at traffic lights go left for Ponthir. In Ponthir cross railway bridge and then river bridge. In 200 yards take turning to right, Candwr Lane. Pass Ponthir House pub on your left. A long but not too hard hill, with several bends, each giving the illusion of being the last before the top. Keep straight on when track narrows (slightly right). A rush down to the valley which appears spread out before you, but beware at the bottom – the road which you join at crossroads is only a minor one but it's surprisingly busy. Turn left. Road is up down up down for 2.5 miles. Turn right for Sôr Brook and Llandegfedd Reservoir. A 1:6 hill down but be warned, there are nasty bends. Cars cut out of Picnic area on left. Cross brook by a narrow bridge, which loses you much of the speed you need for 1:8 hill. The hills down and up are more or less equal length, a mile and a bit each way, but it doesn't seem like it! At T-junction (Give Way) turn left for Llandegfedd Reservoir. The park is open until one hour after sunset. Fine views across the lake to the Black Mountains, Sugar Loaf(1995ft/596m) and Skirrid (The Holy Mountain of Gwent, 1594ft/486m) to NW and Twmbarlwm (1375ft/419m) to SW. Picture board information on wildlife to be found in the area, and explanation of what happens to the water between leaving the lake and reaching taps in Cardiff and Newport.

Leaving the Reservoir, retrace short distance uphill to Coed y Paen. The Carpenters Arms is to your left, a popular pub with local cyclists. Keep on down hill, signed to Llangybi, a twisty road for a mile.

[**Short Ride:** To return to Caerleon, turn right at junction for Llangybi. Climb for three-quarters of a mile then descend for nearly 2 miles – watch your speed as you enter built up area. This is Parc road, you emerge opposite The White Hart. Turn right for Caerleon, 4.5mls/7.25km, or rejoin route of longer ride].

Longer ride: Continue straight ahead at junction, towards Llanbadoc. Pass H.M. Young Offenders Institute on your left and a sawmill on your right. Road climbs with several tight bends, finishing at very awkward junction.

Road from Glascoed joins from your left, and has priority. Keep a keen
ear open as it's tricky to stop on a sharp bit of hill here. Reach Llanbadoc
in one mile, turning left at the T-junction for Usk. St Madoc's church is
on opposite side of road at junction. You may notice that the highway
makes an obvious detour round the church tower, which is on the very
edge of the road. The original road, closed in 1758, is still there, between
the church and the river. In the churchyard there are the steps of an
ancient Cross, with a yew tree in the middle. Arrive in Usk in less than a
mile.

Leaving Usk, retrace route one mile to Llanbadoc, then it's an easy
two miles to Llangybi. The White Hart, a coaching Inn standing on its
own village Green, complete with spreading oak tree, offers Real Ales
and two huge open fireplaces. The church is tucked in behind it. If
you're running out of choccy bars the Post office/shop is a few yards
ahead on the left. Ride for 1.5 miles.

Take minor road to left, almost opposite Cwrt Bleddyn Hotel. Up hill
for half a mile, not too hard. Turn right at crossroads, signed Glen Usk.
At next crossroads with private drive on the right and Croes Llywarch
House on your left, turn left for Llanhennock. Uphill a bit more, then
you're on an ancient Ridgeway between two valleys, with views over
fields and Wentwood Forest that amply reward your efforts. In Llanhennock, the Wheatsheaf Arms, phone box, postbox and church are all on
your left.

On down, all the way from the ridge, a full mile. Look out for road
joining from the left near the bottom and be ready to Give Way at major
road. Turn left for Caerleon and the last drop of downhill run. Turn left
at junction as you enter Caerleon (One-Way). Follow round under Castle
wall and turn back right, through High Street, to Museum. The Roman
Ampitheatre is down the turning to your left, opposite the Museum.

Caerleon

The Roman fortress of Isca at Caerleon was a major military base for
over 200 years. The legionary barracks are the only ones to be seen in
Europe, and the Amphitheatre is the only fully excavated one in Britain.
(Though Chester are working on theirs). It was built about 90 AD with
room for the entire garrison of 6000 people. The Fortress Baths, the
Roman 'Leisure Centre' and swimming pool, were discovered in 1964.

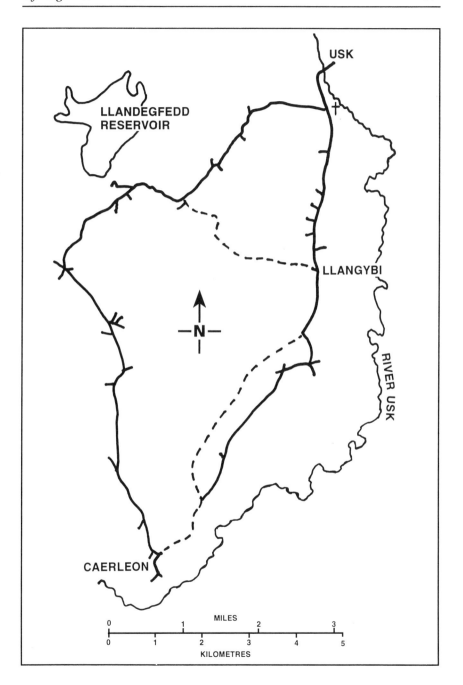

There is a new Museum with an Exhibition illustrating daily life in Roman times, with life-size figures.

Caerleon

Caerleon is believed to have been Camelot, where King Arthur held Court. Tennyson came to the Hanbury Arms to absorb the atmosphere while writing his series of poems on the Arthurian legends, *Idylls of a King*.

Usk

Described in Ride 6.

Tredegar House

Tredegar House, half a mile off the route, is a 17th century stately home with formal state rooms, plus 90 acres of park, gardens and a boating lake. Craft workshops and gift shops, restaurant. Park open all year. House open Easter-September. Tel: (0633) 815880.

8. City Sight-seeing and Rural Rides

Cardiff, Llandaff Cathedral, The Taff and St Fagans.

Distance: 13mls/2lkm.

Longer Option: Continue to Ride 9.

Shorter Option: 8.5mls/15km.

Terrain: Flat alongside river. Longer ride has one moderate climb. Short ride avoids all climbs. River path is earth, sprinkled with fine gravel, can be skid-provoking.

Accommodation/Refreshments/Supplies: Cardiff has all grades of accommodation and eating places. Excellent shopping in old arcades and modern malls. Restaurant and snack bar in Folk Museum. Plymouth Arms in St Fagans village.

Toilets: At many points in Cardiff and in Folk Museum.

Rail Access: Cardiff.

Tourist Information: At Cardiff Station.

Things to see on this Ride: This ride combines a look at the major attractions of the capital of Wales with the peace of the river bank. The route takes you through Cardiff city centre by the quietest and least congested roads. Roundabouts are avoided whenever possible – even if this means taking a roundabout way. Both rides pass Cardiff Castle and Llandaff Cathedral. Longer ride also visits St Fagans Welsh Folk Museum Gardens.

How to Connect with Next Ride: St Fagans is 7mls/11km from Dyffryn Gardens where you may join Ride 9. Go down Castle Hill, over river and railway crossing. Caution – hill is steep and railway is busy – gates are often shut! Climb moderately steep hill for half a mile, to roundabout. Go straight across, (second exit). Take first turning right after the roundabout, Drope Road.

'The Cavalier' pub is on the corner. Pass over the top of dual carriageway. As you descend into St Georges, a picturesque parish church and 'The Greendown Man' pub are on your left, railway to right.

At junction, where road ahead is signed to St Brides, turn left into unmarked lane, which soon becomes a serious hill. Climb for one mile until you reach the A48. Turn right. The next village is St Nicholas. Turn left at traffic lights for Dyffryn Gardens.

The pub in Peterstone Wentlooge, opposite St Peter's church whose six bells were hung in 1722 (see page 34).

Route

Starting Point: Cardiff Central Railway Station. Turn left on leaving Station to ride anti-clockwise round Central Square. At traffic lights go straight across. Wales Empire Pool is on your left.

Follow road round to right, then turn left at traffic lights into Westgate Street. Pass Welsh Rugby Union Ground, universally known as 'The 'Arms Park', on your left. You will soon know if it's a Match day!

Turn right at traffic lights at top of the road, and ride alongside part of the 'Animal Wall' which encloses Bute Park, adjacent to Cardiff Castle. Assorted stone-carved wild birds and beasts crouch on top ready to pounce on passers by.

A quick free glimpse into the Castle Green may be had from the drawbridge. If you're lucky you might see one of the many tame peacocks which roam freely there.

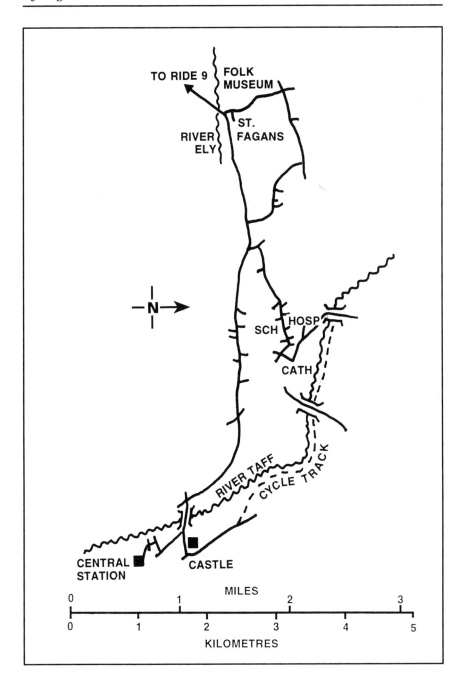

If you wish to leave your bike while sightseeing, there are stands at both ends of Queen Street (a 'pedestrians only' street), and in The Hayes near St David's Hall. It's wise to lock not only the frame but also the wheels to the stand, especially if they're 'quick release' type.

Turn left at the traffic lights by the corner of the Castle and follow round alongside the eastern wall with its grassed over moat. The imposing buildings of Portland stone which comprise Cardiff's Civic Centre – Law Courts, City Hall and National Museum of Wales – can be seen to your right, the other side of a junction.

Keep straight ahead until the pedestrian-controlled lights, by the Welsh College of Music and Drama on your left. Here you pick up a cycle/pedestrian track, initially through a car park. Go past the Ambulance station and through the gate – the first of a series of obstructions. Designed to keep motorbikes and horseriders off the track, these are a considerable nuisance to a loaded touring bike. When the track divides take the left fork alongside the river, signed 'Taff Trail to Castell Coch'. Go under the first road bridge, keeping to the left and following the river. The spire of Llandaff Cathedral can be seen above the trees on the opposite bank. Pass the Weir and continue to the second bridge. There are steps up to the road but you may find it easier to go through the tunnel and then push your bike over the grass up the short incline on the right-hand side. Ride back over the bridge.

Go left at the mini-roundabout and take first left immediately after passing the 'Heathcock' pub, into Bridge Street, leading to The Green and Llandaff Cathedral.

Continue past the Cathedral and down Llandaff High Street. At the T-junction turn right into Cardiff Road. Near top of hill, at the traffic lights, take first left into Fairwater Road. Continue in Fairwater Road when it forks left after 400 yards. Pass Cantonian High School on your left, and near the bottom of the hill, the Ski Centre on your right. Turn left at a T-junction, continue to traffic lights 150 yards ahead.

(Short ride turns left here, where an old-style finger post points 'To Ely'. Follow 'short ride continues here' instructions at end of ride).

Turn right at the traffic lights into St Fagans Road. Climb gradually for half a mile, then descend into St Fagans.

There is an entrance to the Welsh Folk Museum opposite you. Use this entrance for preference – the main entrance, at the bottom of Castle Hill, is through the car park.

To return to Cardiff:

Leave Folk Museum by the same gate, at the top of the hill, and turn left. St Mary's church is opposite. Pass Plymouth Arms on your right. Ride for half a mile, leaving village behind. At crossroads, turn right into narrow country road, Pentrebane Road. Ride for one mile.

As you enter built up area, take right turn signed to 'Pentrebane Community Centre'. (Beechley Drive). Pass school, shops and Community Centre. Start downhill, riding beside a strip of railed park, and take next turning on right into Gorse Place, with railings on the left. Ride to T-junction at end of road and turn left. In 400 yards you are back at traffic lights in Fairwater. Go straight ahead.

(Short ride continues here.) After half a mile, go under a railway bridge and straight over at traffic lights where Waugron Road crosses Western Avenue. There is a short section of divided carriageway, followed by more traffic lights. Go straight across into Pencisely Road, a quiet residential road. Ride one mile, go straight across at traffic lights into Penhill Road. Bear right at bottom of hill. This is Cathedral Road, a wide tree-lined avenue of grand Victorian houses, mostly guest houses or doctors' premises. At end of road turn left at traffic lights (filter) and cross bridge over the River Taff. Turn right at traffic lights into Westgate Street to return to Station.

Cardiff

Cardiff Castle has a Roman Wall, a Norman Keep with Moat, a Clock Tower 150ft high, an extensive Green with peacocks and a military Museum. Guided Tours are available. The National Museum of Wales can show you dinosaur footprints found recently near Barry, a coal mine, and many fascinating Exhibitions. The Art Gallery has recently had a new wing added and is home to many major works.

Llandaff Cathedral is built on a site first used by St Teilo nearly 1500 years ago. Epstein's renowned sculpture, 'Christ in Majesty' dominates the interior.

St Fagans Welsh Folk Museum: This open-air Museum in 50 acres of beautifully landscaped grounds allows you to experience the social life of Wales from the 16th century through to modern times. Saddlers, potters and weavers can be watched as they pursue their crafts. More than 30 buildings, timber farmhouses from the 1500s and 1600s, a strange circular pig-sty and a whole terrace of workers' cottages are laid out. Native livestock, Welsh Black cattle, Welsh mountain sheep and traditional breeds of poultry can also be seen.

9. A Seaside Saint and a Welsh Country Garden

Barry – Dyffryn Gardens – Barry

Distance: 14.5mls/24km.

Longer Option: To continue to Llantwit Major, do Ride 10 and return to Barry, would total 49mls/79km.

Terrain: Only moderate hills. None longer than half a mile.

Accommodation/Refreshments/Supplies: Limited choice of accommodation in Barry. Hotels at Cardiff Wales Airport (Rhoose) close to route. Cafes at Barry Island (mostly in summer) and in Dyffryn Gardens from Easter to October. Shops and supermarkets in Barry.

Toilets: Barry Island and Dyffryn Gardens.

Rail Access: Barry (Valley Lines).

Things to see on this Ride: Barry Island Resort. St Baruch's Chapel. Roman Villa. Dyffryn Gardens. (Open all year). Tinkinswood and St Lythans ancient Burial Chambers.

How to Connect to Next Ride: Exit from Dyffryn Gardens to the right. Right at junction. Take next turning right. At crossroads with Five Mile Lane, straight across, steeply down to Llancarfan. Cross shallow ford. If there's a loaded tractor stationary in the water, it isn't stuck. It has a rendez-vous with another tractor. It's easier for them to pass in the ford as the river is wider than the road.

Turn left after the ford, up the hill (one that's on my personal hate-list) and right at the top. The building dominating the skyline is a British Airways Maintenance hangar. After half a mile, left at fork, by large farmhouse and grassy triangle. Through Treguff. A steep drop for a mile and a climb out. In 1.4 miles, go left at crossroads and keep straight on for Llantwit Major. 9mls/14.5km.

Route

Starting Point: Barry Railway Station. Turn left out of station and left at junction, One-Way, signed Barry Island. Downhill and left at bottom to ride over causeway past old harbour. Keep straight on when car park is

signed to left, into Roman Well Road. The name is all that remains of a
Well which older inhabitants remember – it has now been built over.
Fun fair on right. Barry Island railway station on your left. Continue
until road ahead is signed Dead End. Turn right and go straight on
when road bears left, into Friars Road, another Dead End.

On the left, overlooking breakwater and Docks entrance, wedged
between the road and the cliff edge, you can see the remains of St
Baruch's Chapel. St Baruch, who gave his name to Barry, was drowned
off the coast in 700 AD. He was once so famous that his shrine was a
place of pilgrimage, and in medieval times the faithful requested that
they should be buried nearby.

Victorian buildings on Barry Island often show elaborate wrought-iron
balconies, a style which looks old-fashioned here, but which was much
copied in Australia.

Leaving the Chapel, start back the way you came but turn left to pass
in front of the holiday camp, and ride parallel to the sea front. Whitmore
Bay is a popular sandy beach, with views over the Somerset coast.
Cycling is not allowed on the promenade. Complete circuit of island and
return over causeway.

Turn left at end of causeway into The Parade, with gardens on your
left. At the end of The Parade, turn right, and then make a U-turn left.
Pass a few shops and follow round mini-roundabout to Promenade. At
the entrance to the car terrace, look for path rising to your right, beyond
public toilet block. (You will have to walk this bit). A large Roman
building, dated AD 400-and-something, has been excavated here. There
is a viewing platform and display boards explaining the layout of almost
a score of rooms.

A couple of miles along the coast, rocks imprinted with a group of
dinosaurs' footprints were discovered, only a few years ago. They can be
seen in the Geology department of National Museum of Wales in
Cardiff.

Return past shops and continue under railway arch. Immediately turn
left, up hill, opposite Romilly Park. When road forks, keep left to reach
top of hill. A very steep finish. Turn left at a T-junction and right at next
fork to pass between church on left and Barry Castle ruins on right. This
dainty Castle has been tidied up and prettified with flowers. Beyond the
Castle, and post office on your left, turn right into Oxford Street, a
lengthy residential street which later becomes Salisbury road. At T-

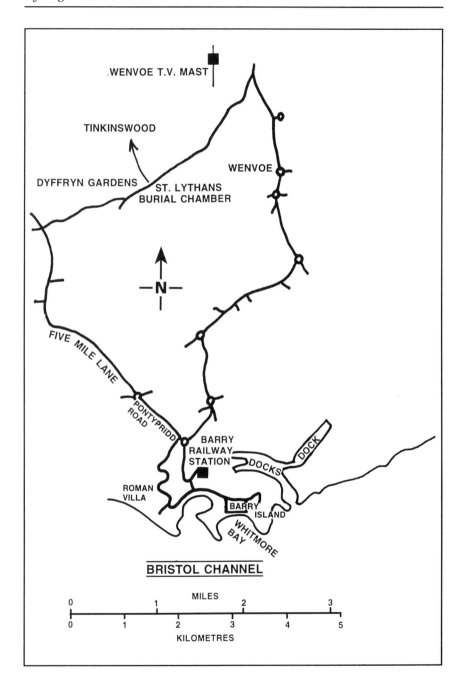

WENVOE T.V. MAST

TINKINSWOOD

DYFFRYN GARDENS

WENVOE

ST. LYTHANS
BURIAL CHAMBER

—N—

FIVE MILE LANE

PONTYPRIDD ROAD

BARRY
RAILWAY
STATION

DOCK

DOCKS

ROMAN
VILLA

BARRY
ISLAND

WHITMORE BAY

BRISTOL CHANNEL

MILES
0   1   2   3
0   1   2   3   4   5
KILOMETRES

junction turn left into Pontypridd road, and ride down to roundabout. Take second exit into Weycock Road, commonly known as '5-Mile Lane'. An undulating country road, there's an initial run down. The Welsh Hawking Centre is on the right at the bottom. A moderately steep climb up from the stream with a plantation on your left.

If you need reviving, The Three Horseshoes is a couple of hundred yards down the turning to the left, signed to Moulton.

Halfway down Five Mile Lane, take second turning right, at offset crossroads, to Dyffryn. The lane runs downhill between high hedges for a mile, past a farm, and ends at a bridge. Turn left at a T-junction, climb gently for half a mile and take next turning left. Dyffryn Gardens are a quarter of a mile down on the left. (Return to this point later).

Half a mile beyond Dyffryn on your left, is a 'kissing' gate and a sign pointing the way to Tinkinswood Burial Chamber, two fields from the road (people coming from Cardiff pass it on their right).

Go back to the junction given above. Turn left, signed Cardiff, and in 200 yards an 'Ancient Monument' sign on the right indicates St Lythans burial chamber, close to the road.

From here the road descends to the valley bottom, then climbs away again to St Lythans village. The Wenvoe HTV mast is on the left. The Horse and Jockey is set back from the road, just before an extremely sharp corner. Extra care is needed going down the hill. There's a concealed exit for heavy lorries a short way beyond the double bend.

Before the bottom of the hill, take acute-angled turn to right – it's a shame to have to check your speed, but there's more downhill to come. Pay attention though – run ends at a Give Way sign.

Go straight across junction, through Wenvoe village, with pub, church and shops, and a fine avenue of conker trees. Right at roundabout, then straight across next one and take second exit at the third.

Pass Barry/Barri town sign and go left at roundabout into Colcot Road, with Colcot Arms on your left. Ride down wide residential road for one mile. Straight on at roundabout, following sign to Barry Island. Road bears right, with views over coast to your left. (Jenner Road).

Straight across (first exit) at next roundabout into Park Crescent, a shopping street. Straight on at crossroads between two churches, into St Nicholas Road. Downhill, but take care, there's a junction before the end of the hill. Turn left at junction and keep left, following 'Town Centre' sign into One-Way section. Barry station is 200 yards on your right.

Barry Island

A traditional family holiday resort. Whitmore Bay is a fine sandy bay with fast-food, fairy lights and general razzamatazz.

Welsh Hawking Centre

Over 250 Birds of Prey to be seen. Flying displays. Children's play area and pony rides. Open every day. Cafe in summer.

Dyffryn Gardens

These landscaped gardens with rare and exotic plants and trees are beautifully laid out. The heir to the original owner of Dyffryn House was an expert horticulturist. The rockeries, heather gardens, statuary, ornamental fountains and lawns are a delight.

Gardens open all year. House closed to the public. Tearooms, Easter to October. Toilets. Tel: 0222 593328.

Llantwit Major Cycling Club, near Dyffryn Gardens. 11--year-old Kelly (on the tandem) is an experienced cyclist.

Tinkinswood Burial Chamber

It's amazingly big – the capstone possibly the biggest in Britain with an estimated weight of 40 tons. It's amazingly old – built about 4000 BC in the Stone Age. The 'primitive' people of those times took enormous pains to respect their dead. It would have needed the skilful co-operation of a couple of hundred men to raise that massive slab. The bones of a group of 40 or 50 people, men, women and children, were found here.

St Lythan's Burial Chamber

Smaller than Tinkinswood, but still impressive, this tomb dates from about the same period. It is the type classified as 'Cotswold/Severn', following the pattern of a culture established in the Cotswolds. The recognisable features of this style of burial chamber are the wedge shape, and a forecourt with a chamber opening off, facing East.

St Lythan's Neolithic Long Cairn, near Dyffryn Gardens

10. Stepping Stones

Llantwit Major – Llandow – Castle-Upon-Alun – St Brides Major – Ogmore – Nash Point – St Donats – Llantwit Major.

Distance: 31mls/50km

Shorter Options: Returning from St Brides reduces ride by 6mls/10km. Leaving out Nash Point saves 2mls/3km.

Terrain: Undulating. No alarming hills.

Accommodation/Refreshments/Supplies: A Country Hotel, pubs, supermarket and shops in Llantwit. Farmers Arms at St Brides. Shops and The Pelican at Ogmore.

Toilets: In car park in Llantwit Major.

Rail Access: Barry 9mls/14.4km E. Bridgend 10mls/16km NW.

Tourist Information: Small office in Town Hall Llantwit.

Things to see on this Ride: Llantwit Major – historic town, St Illtud's 13th century church. Nash Point Iron Age hillfort, Lighthouse. Glamorgan Heritage Coast. St Donat's Castle and Arts Centre.

How to Connect with Next Rides: At junction with the B4265 near Ogmore, marked LINK NOTE in text, continue to Ewenny. (Ewenny Priory, medieval monastic site, Romanesque church, is off the route, about a mile ahead on the south side of the river). Cross river Ogmore and immediately turn left (signed Merthyr Mawr and Laleston).

Continue towards Laleston at crossroads. Over humpbacked bridge. Turn left on A48 and take next turning to right (200 yards). Straight across A473. Left at junction, then quickly right. At bottom of hill keep left at junction signed Kenfig Hill. Right at crossroads. Pass under the M4.

At crossroads in Cefn Cribwr go straight ahead, crossing B4281. Steep hill down (12%). Ride over re-developed opencast mining area. In Ffordd-y-Gyfraith go straight on, (right/left) at offset crossroads and begin hard climb, to top. Right at T-junction to arrive in Llangynwyd by the Cross with Old House/Hen Dŷ pub on right. 19mls/32km.

Route

Starting Point: Begin from the car park behind the Old Town Hall in the centre of the old part of town, above the church. A good view over the town from the terrace.

Exit to right from car park, into The Strand. This is a complicated junction, where three narrow and congested streets converge. (Street names in Llantwit change every few yards. The Strand follows on from Church Lane. Commercial Street becomes High Street). Go left past Barclays Bank into High Street, pass St Illtyd's Primary School on your right, and bear left into Turkey Street. (One-Way). Continue to irregular crossroads and go straight on, with a little twist to the left. (A little way down Turkey Street, there's a Ford on your left, with a rough bed to the stream, if you want to cross for the fun of it. Or you can use the footbridge, which is enough of a challenge with loaded panniers. A bit of a Castle and 'The Old Place' are back to the left on the opposite side, but go right to rejoin the route at the crossroads). Over to your right you may catch sight of The Great House, a Tudor Manor House, now carefully restored.

Wick road was formerly the main road to Bridgend. Ride clear of the town for a mile, past Purlon Farm on corner on left. At main road, briefly turn left, cross over and immediately turn right into small road which passes under railway bridge alongside the main road. Enter a lane which is used by farm traffic and can be dirty in bad weather.

After one mile, turn left opposite World War 2 hangars, and ride by security fence. Take next turning right, signed to 'Civic Amenity Site'. Crossing the disused Llandow airfield, you come to a T-junction with an old runway straight in front of you, the other side of the fence. Turn left, pass Llandow Trading Estate.

In about a mile, at a T-junction, turn right, signs to Colwinston and Cowbridge. Turn left at next junction. Straight on at crossroads, ride for two and a half miles.

Notice the turning to Colwinston, which is on your right, with signpost which is on your left. The turning you want is 0.3m from here, on your left. It's easy to miss. There's a farm gate into a field opposite but otherwise no identifying features. If you do miss it you can still reach the same point via the next turning. The road bends downhill

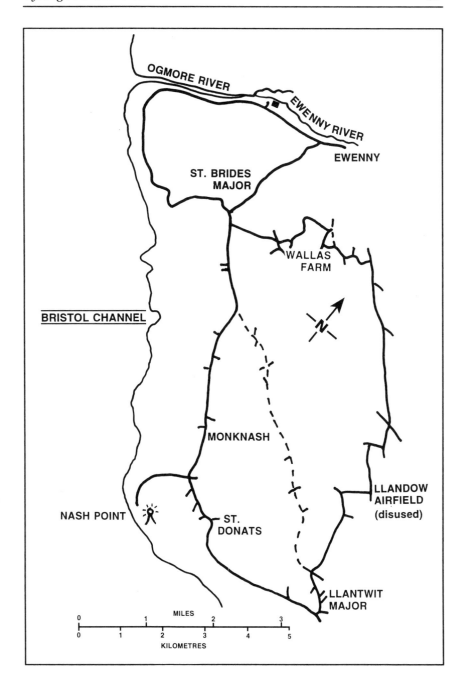

OGMORE RIVER

EWENNY RIVER

EWENNY

ST. BRIDES
MAJOR

WALLAS
FARM

BRISTOL CHANNEL

N

MONKNASH

LLANDOW
AIRFIELD
(disused)

NASH POINT

ST.
DONATS

LLANTWIT
MAJOR

MILES
0   1   2   3
0   1   2   3   4   5
KILOMETRES

through Lampha village. Keep on to T-junction opposite a large stone farmhouse (Wallas Farm). Turn right, and in a quarter of a mile, turn left, at an off-set crossroads where the righthand turning is an unmade track. There's a high stone wall on the corner. The slope's an inducement to let rip, but don't overdo it – the road ends in the river, the Afon Alun. The water level varies from bone dry to a couple of feet or more. It's a wide ford. When it's deep, it needs an exhilarating degree of speed to fly through in a cloud of spray. If you run out of speed, it's instinctive to start pedalling, but Don't Do It! You'll find yourself deposited full length in the stream. (personal experience talking here). If you prefer discretion to valour, there are stepping stones.

Safely over, follow lane up the other side. At the top, go straight across slightly offset crossroads and carry on until you see the swans in St Bride's pond. The Farmers Arms is on your left. Turn right, ride alongside pond and turn left at next corner by War Memorial.

(**Short Ride:** turn left past Farmers' Arms and omit next four paragraphs.)

Go through Southerndown, past Three Golden Cups on right. Climb, initially away from the sea, then turn parallel to coast. Soon you're on a cliff top with very little between you and the sea. Enjoyable views of the coast and the Exmoor Hills, and Sker Point to your right. At some stages of the tide, Tusker Rock can be seen, about a mile out to sea, as you ride beside the common. This stretch of coast was infamous for wreckers and smugglers until quite recent times.

Watch out for cattle grids at both ends of common. Go through Ogmore. Road bears right and follows the river Ogmore upstream. After a mile and a bit, Ogmore Castle is on your left, opposite The Pelican Inn.

After viewing the stepping stones – see next page – and Castle, return to the road and in 1.5 miles turn right at awkward junction, following the B4265, signed to Llantwit Major.

LINK NOTE: Leave Ride here if you wish to continue to Next Ride.

Climb through a steep-sided valley, the sides glowing with gorse most of the year. Cattle grids each end of the valley, and the very big Pant quarry on the right. Re-enter St Brides. Pass the Fox and Hounds and later the Farmers Arms where you were earlier. This time keep straight on, climbing gradually.

Stepping Stones, River Ogmore

Llantwit Major is straight ahead if you want the shortest road, but a prettier and less busy way is to take the right turn signed to Monknash and Marcross, just over a mile from St Brides. There are good pubs at both places.

After three miles there's a right turn by the Horseshoe Inn to Nash Point Lighthouse. It's an attractive run beside a chine for one mile, with views of an Iron Age Hill Fort, 700 BC to AD 100, one of a line of similar defences strung along the coast from Barry to Bridgend. No cycling beyond the car park but you can walk round the lighthouse.

To continue, return to the Horseshoe Inn and turn right. A sudden spiteful little hill here. A mile further on, after a sharp corner, is St Donat's Castle. Keep right on entering Llantwit Major to return to church.

Llantwit Major/Llanilltud Fawr

Llantwit Major was the oldest University town in Britain, famous long before Oxford. Its monastery, church and school were flourishing about

400 AD. It's widely believed that St David was a pupil here. The names Wine Street, Turkey Street, and Baker Lane are a legacy of the 16th and 17th centuries. The Town Hall is 15th century and the Old Swan inn, 16th century. Castle Ditches, an Iron Age hill fort, can be seen from the beach road through Col Huw valley. The church has a fine collection of Early Christian sculptured stone crosses. Best to visit the church before setting off, as it's to one side of the route. Even people not normally interested in churches find this one quite out of the ordinary. Worth seeing too, is the astonishingly complete 13th century dovecote, attached to a ruined medieval Grange, to the west of the church. From Burial Lane, follow the boundary of back of church, as far as a footpath with steps up. To avoid these, go right and double back left, up short steep hill. Go right into lane, and dovecote can be seen from gateway on your left. A footpath gives access to it.

Llandow

Hundreds of pilots of many nations learned to fly the legendary Spitfire from this airfield between 1941 and 1943. In 1945 there was a mass escape of German P.O.W.s from nearby Bridgend, and some were captured hiding here.

Ogmore Castle

A 12th – 14th century castle, by a ford marked by ancient stepping stones.

St Donat's Castle

St Donat's once belonged to William Randolph Hearst, the American newspaper tycoon, who did a lot of restoration work. In 1962 it opened as an International Sixth Form school. The Arts centre in a converted tithe-barn puts on a variety of concerts and plays. The Castle is sometimes open to the public during the summer holidays.

11. Cycle Trails and Fairyland tales.
An ancient abbey, and an ancient pub

Afan Argoed, Margam Park, Hen Dŷ

Distance: 31mls/50km

Longer Option: To connect with Ride 12, ride it and return would amount to about 85mls/137km altogether.

Shorter Options: Returning to Maesteg from Bryn would give a ride of 12mls/20km. Circuits within the Country Park from 10mls/16km to 18mls/29km.

Terrain: One moderate hill and one whopper. Easy going inside the Park.

Accommodation/Refreshments/Supplies: For help in finding accommodation, contact Vale of Neath Hoteliers' Association, Castle Hotel. Tel: 0639 721795. Excellent caféteria at Afan Argoed. Two cafés at Margam Park. Hen Dŷ pub. Shops in Maesteg.

Toilets: At Afan Argoed and Margam Park.

Rail Access: Port Talbot main line, 7mls. Maesteg links with Bridgend for London – Swansea line.

Tourist Information: At Afan Argoed and Margam Park.

Things to see on this Ride: Afan Argoed Country Park. Cycle Centre, with circuit of Forestry Commission tracks. River views. Margam Park, deer park, Orangery, Medieval Abbey, Maze, Fairytale land for young children. Hen Dŷ – one of the oldest pubs in Wales, dates back over 800 years and still offers Real Ale.

How to Connect with Next Ride: To join Ride 12 from the Lliw reservoir – From Pontrhydyfen, take the B4287 to Neath. Neath Abbey, 12th – 16th century, was once described as 'the Fairest Abbey in All Wales' – a rival to Tintern standing in a similarly tranquil environment. Although very much a ruin, and difficult to disentangle from its industrial surroundings, the elegance and grandeur of the architecture can still be appreciated. Take the B4291 through Birchgrove to Clydach. Then via Craig-Cefn-Parc and Rhyd-y-Pandy to the Lower Lliw Reservoir. 17mls/27km.

Route

From Afan Argoed Country Park, turn West on the A4107 and follow river downstream for 3.5mls/5.6km. Be ready to change to low gear very smartly as you switch from downhill to climb, on left-hand turn to join the B4282, signed Maesteg. Watch the mirror if you swing out.

(If you're having a short ride, continue on this road to Maesteg. Leave Maesteg to the North on the A4063 to Caerau and follow description from there back to Afan Argoed).

Continue for two miles to Bryn. Just before a rise, on entering the village, take Chapel Terrace down to the right, turning right across stream at bottom of hill. A narrow lane winds with the stream for 2.5 miles before widening out by Goytre cemetery. Pass under M4 to join the A48 opposite Taibach post office.

Turn left and ride through built-up area for 2 miles, to roundabout. Don't panic at signs which appear to indicate that you're committed to the motorway. Ride towards Cardiff on a dual carriageway for 400 yards to next roundabout, pass over M4 and keep left on the A48. First left is the entrance to Margam Abbey, founded 1147 AD, 'Stones' Museum of Early Christian (5th century onwards) Standing Stones and Burial Stones, and The Abbots Kitchen cafeteria. *NB. This is not the Country Park Entrance, which is half a mile further on, on the left.*

Leaving Margam Park, turn left towards Pyle. Ride for 2.4 miles, take left turn signed to Pen y Bryn. It's easy to miss – if you see 'Welcome to Mid-Glamorgan' you've come too far.

A moderate hill for three quarters of a mile, and a couple of miles of rolling country before a left turn to Llangwyndd, marked 'Narrow road unsuitable for Heavy Vehicles'. This lane is steep and narrow in an almost Biblical fashion – why are steep and narrow pathways harder than the merely steep? It's an unremarkable mile long, but feels longer. At the top is the well-deserved view, before a full measure of compensation by way of a two mile plunge downhill.

The church tower and a large graveyard can be seen dominating their small village. Turn right on the run-out and it's a short rise to Llangynwyd. The Corner House pub is on your left, a Celtic Cross ahead of you, and Yr Hen Dŷ – The Old House – opposite.

Leave Llangynwyd from the Cross, taking the road up the hill with

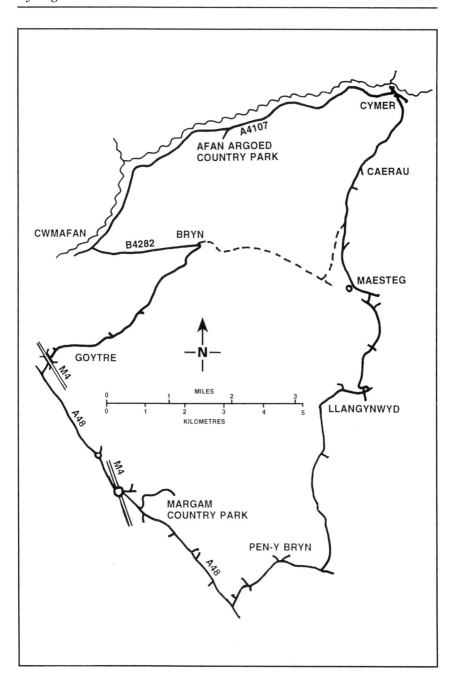

the churchyard on your right and Corner House on your left. Turn left at the top, signed to Cwmfelin, three quarters of a mile. It's all downhill and you probably won't notice much about Cwmfelin. Left for Maesteg on the A4063 at the bottom. In centre of Maesteg turn right at traffic lights, signed to Nantyffyllon and Caerau, and left at next traffic lights, signed Nantyffyllon one mile. Go through both of them, they're continuous. Keep left in Caerau, signed to Cymmer, 2.5 miles.

Don't look up at the traffic apparently suspended in the heavens, it might discourage you. Halfway up hill, downhill traffic is warned to stay in a low gear. No problem for you – you're probably pushing the lever in hope of finding a gear lower than your lowest.

Over the hill, round the corner, and it's down to Cymmer. Join the Port Talbot road at the bottom and run the 3 miles down the valley to Afan Argoed, or if you prefer, pick up the circuit in the Country Park here. (Turn right at clocktower).

Afan Argoed Country Park

Within the Park an attractive circuit of 10m/16km of track has been constructed, out along one side of the river and back via the other. This can be extended by a few miles at each end of the valley. You can take your own bike on the track. It's O.K. for tourers but a bit flinty in patches, or you can hire Mountain Bike from the Centre. (2 forms of ID needed but credit cards not accepted). Hired bikes must not leave Park, but there are many opportunities for off-road riding for mountain bikers in the area around Afan Argoed. Ask the Forestry Commission for details.

Visitors Centre with shop, Miners' Museum (entry charge) and free Exhibition of Natural History in the Park. Caféteria. Tel: (0639) 850564.

Margam Park

800 acres of parkland, two lakes, a mile of maze. Plus farm trails, Fairytale Land and entertainment for families. Iron Age Hill Fort. Cistercian Abbey, 1147 AD (ruins). Celebrated Orangery over 100 yards long. Built in 1789 and now used for craft fairs and various exhibitions throughout the year. Cafés open daily April to September. Limited opening time in winter. Tel: (0639) 871131.

12. A Tour of Many Mynydds
The Lliw Valley

Distance: 19.5mls/31km

Longer Options: Ride on to Swansea and the Gower, which has many options.

Shorter Options: No short options. A showing-off ride, though not a long one. Once you start you may as well finish – as Macbeth put it, 'returning were as tedious as go o'er.'

Terrain: Not for children or persons of faint-hearted disposition.

Accommodation/Refreshments/Supplies: For accommodation see under Rides II or 13. Small café at Reservoir, for hot drinks and replenishing stocks of chocolate. Scotch Pine Pub at the summit.

Toilets: At the Reservoir.

Rail Access/Car Parking: Swansea station 14mls/22.5km. Free car park at Reservoir, 8 am to dusk.

Things to see on this Ride: Typical Welsh mountain scenery. If you have only a short time in Wales, this ride captures the essence. Anything moving on the road is a sheep and the loudest sound is a grasshopper. **NB** Keep this ride for a fine day. It's a high, exposed route without shelter.

How to Connect with Next Ride: To Swansea, 9mls/14.4km. From the Masons' Arms take road signed to Morriston/Trefors. (Rhyd-y-Pandy road). Go under M4 and turn right, then at roundabout first left, for the B4489. This joins the A418 a quarter of a mile from Swansea Station.

Route

Starting Point: SE tip of Lower Lliw Reservoir (SN 651034). At the end of the access road from the Reservoir, turn left, following sign to Rhyd-y-pandy. Keep left at Masons Arms and left at next junction. Begin ascent which will continue for 5 miles, not entirely unalleviated – there are easements of 20 yards or so which are much appreciated, and even a definite drop, but in general the way is UP.

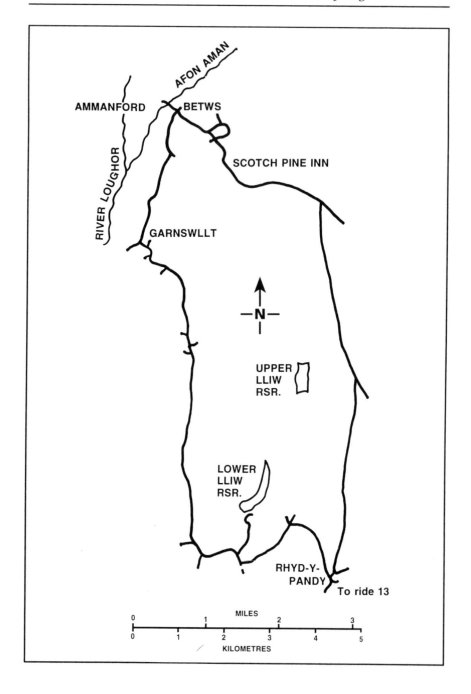

As your wheels roll over the summit and find themselves momentarily on level ground, the view spread before you shows wooded valleys, small, stranded farms, and the road disappearing over the next hill. The Scotch Pine is on your right if you need refreshment.

Before you let rip down the hill, beware of a cattle grid. A steep descent for 2 miles, unfortunately with a lot of bends – not the comfortable Alpine type of hairpin but tight blind corners. Check your rims don't get too hot.

Just before the bottom, as the houses begin, go left into Fford Waun Gron. Continue down to crossroads, with Post box on your right opposite. Left here through Betws. Pass sign 'Borough of Lliw valley'. There's a sharp left-hand corner as you enter Garnswllt, but only one way to go, other way is dead-end.

Shortly after passing a phone box on your left, road divides. Leave Pontardulais road and take left fork, up hill, into unsigned minor road. Both roads are marked as unsuitable for heavy traffic.

You're now on a mountain road. Pen-y-Gors pub is on your left. A local woman described the route from here as 'uphill, mind, that's the way of it – then down a bit, then over another mountain – and, well, like that'. Switchback movements of her hands said it all. But eventually it's clear that you've passed the peak. The final hill down is a 1 in 4 and brings you right to Felindre village.

Go left, uphill once more, and left to the reservoir.

13. A Girdle round the Gower (squeezing in all the best bits)

Swansea – Mumbles – Gower Peninsula – Swansea

Distance: 55mls/88.5km

Options: The route goes all the way to the far west of the Gower peninsular, but there are an almost infinite number of points from which it's simple to complete a smaller loop. To Mumbles and back would be 16mls/26km. Returning from Parkmill 24mls/38km. Returning from Fairyhill 38mls/61km

Terrain: Swansea Bay to Mumbles is flat. On Gower the hills are nasty, brutish and short. There are lots of them but most are no more than half a mile long.

Accommodation/Refreshments/Supplies: Plenty of choice in Swansea/Mumbles, especially small hotels and Guest Houses along the bay. Cafe at Mumbles. Pubs in Bishopston, Kittle, Llanrhidian, Reynoldston, Oxwich, Rhossili and Scurlage. Kiosks at Caswell Bay, Oxwich and Rhossili in summer. Good shop for picnic supplies at Parkmill. Youth Hostel at Port-Eynon.

Toilets: Two locations on Swansea Bike Path. Caswell Bay. Oxwich.

Rail Access: Swansea.

Things to see on this Ride: Coastal and moorland scenery. Golden beaches. Weobley Castle. Rhossili Norman church. King Arthur's Stone. (Off the road).

How to Connect with Next Rides: The Clyne Valley bike path extends northwards from the Railway Pub near Killay, but deteriorates after 2 miles into a track too rough for touring biikes. Join B4296 (Cecil Road) and continue to Gowerton. Go straight across traffic lights and take next right – Pont-y-Cob (Bridge of the Embankment) also loosely called the Marsh Road. You have to join the new A484 trunk road to cross the Loughor Bridge. If you want to stay with it to Llanelli, it's a flat smooth road with a hard shoulder to ride on, but I don't like traffic. Turn off right for the old road. Leave Llanelli on B4309. It's a hilly ride to Pontyates and on to Cwmffrwd. Turn left on to A40. 8 miles on the A40 or 12 miles navigating through Llangynog. (Real ale at Wern Inn here). In St. Clears turn left on A4066 for Laugharne. 40mls/64kms.

Route

Starting Point: Swansea Railway Station.

Cross over road (traffic lights) into turning which makes a cross-roads with the station yard, and follow signs to Gower, the A4118. Go left at next traffic lights (filter), signed City Centre, on dual carriage way road. Straight on at roundabout, downhill. Get into right-hand lane and turn right, into dual carriage way road, with the Leisure Centre on your left. Pass large 'Pay and Display' car park, then County Hall on your left, Swansea jail on your right. Four sets of traffic lights along this section.

Look out for sloping access way to bike path on your left, three-quarters of a mile from the Leisure Centre, opposite Bath Hotel. There's no sign for it.

The path is shared between cyclists and pedestrians, the latter have priority and bikes are not always popular with the families and older people who crowd both ends of the track on summer weekends. The middle section is usually clear. The bike path has some tricky bits – just past the University, turn smartly left or you'll be funnelled into a car park.

When the tide's up, you ride with the water smacking the sea wall and promising to spray your pedals. When its out, it all but vanishes. Both ways, it's a soothing five-mile ride.

As you approach Mumbles, there are lines of guest houses and family hotels all along the front. Toilets here, where the shopping street joins the promenade.

The pier is half a mile further on from the Lifeboat Station, along a subsidiary road with speed humps. By the pier you find 'amusements', a bar, cafés and toilets – the last two not always open out of season.

Go back to the Lifeboat station and join the B4433 to ride up Mumbles Hill and round the headland. In autumn the Look Out by the coastguard station is a vantage point for observing thousands of migratory birds as they set off from Britain. Ride along overlooking the sea, turning right at the bottom of the hill. Up hill, through a housing area, and into a narrow lane for 200 yards, emerging into a residential road, below a caravan site.

Keep left into Higher Lane. Road narrows at top of hill into another short stretch of single track road. Pass some houses and begin a descent

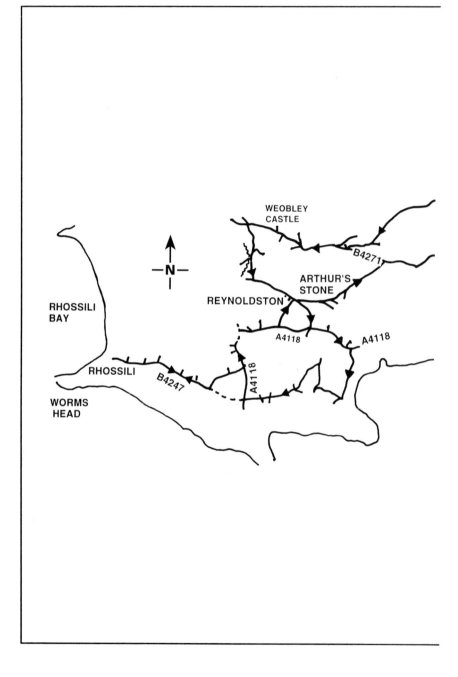

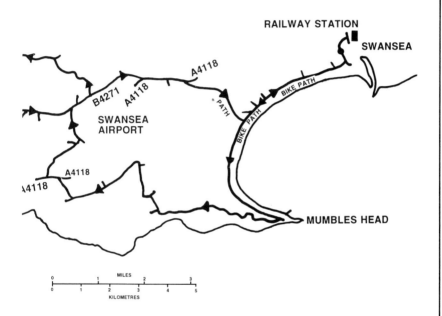

RAILWAY STATION

SWANSEA

A4118

B4271

A4118

BIKE PATH

PATH

BIKE PATH

SWANSEA
AIRPORT

A4118

44118

MUMBLES HEAD

MILES
0   1   2   3
0   1   2   3   4   5
KILOMETRES

with golf course to your left. Over a bridge, and after 50 yards of divided carriageway, go left at the T-junction changing immediately to going uphill. Follow signs to Gower and Caswell Bay, and keep right where sign indicates Caswell. There's a right-left turn around St Peters church. As Caswell Road begins to go down hill, a plaque on the wall to your right records the fact that Frances Ridley Havergal, who died in 1879, lived here. She was known as a 'Christian poetess and hymn writer.'

A steep descent now. The opposite side of the valley rises up to hit you in the face. On the way down pass holiday chalets, then the Bishop's Wood Country Centre on your left, with the Glamorgan Wild Life Trust shop, open weekends in summer.

At the foot of the hill, an unexpected 'Keep Left' sign can catch you unawares. There are toilets in the car park opposite. Climb up the hill you saw as you came down. It's quite a pull. Pass footpath to Brandy Cove. In Bishopston turn left into Pyle Road. There's a Post Office and stores on the corner here. Bishopston is a long sprawling village. Past the school, there's a pub both sides – the Joiners Arms to your left and Bishopston Valley on your right.

Ford beside Bishopston (Church Road), just off-route

Turn left at the T-junction with the B4436, sign-posted to Port Eynon and Pennard. Go up the hill into Kittle. There's a shop on the left and the Beaufort Arms pub, circa 1460, on the right, also post office and store.

In Pennard go straight ahead into 'Dead End' road signed Southgate when main road turns right to South Gower. Entering a built-up area, pass 30 mph speed limit sign, and school. Take right turn by phone box, Linkside Drive.

Wend your way through the residential streets, keeping in Linkside Drive. Left at shop and on down until you come to what appears to be a dead-end with a gate ahead, at junction with Norton Drive. This is a narrow road with a neglected but acceptable surface. Turn left, go steeply down, cross stream and turn left on the A4118.

The Post Office and shop are on your right. Take the road immediately in front of the shop to visit a working corn mill, dating from the 1300s, a 19th century sawmill, and a craft shop with hand-carved wooden articles. There is also a picnic area, embellished with a pillory, and a stream. Toilets available to visitors. On leaving, cross ford and turn left, or return the way you came, to the shop.

Take steep uphill turning, behind the shop, signposted to Lunnon and Ilston. This is an awkward climb from a standing start. Turn right in Lunnon, round Lunnon Farm.

[The ride can be made a few miles shorter by going straight on here to Llanrhidian, but it's a plainer route].

Ride downhill to Ilston, and over stream. The road crosses a common. Turn right at a T-junction with the B4271.

[To end the ride, continue on this road and rejoin route at Upper Killay.]

In half a mile, take left turn signed Cilonen. Ride for 1.5 miles across the common, watching out for loose livestock, then left at a T-junction by Cilonen Road sign. This is a quiet road between high hedges, with occasional glimpses of the Loughor estuary. Keep straight on towards Llanrhidian, coming out onto the open moorland known as 'Welsh Moor'. A pretty run with the road bordered by rushes. There are views right across the peninsular in one direction, and of the escarpment and marshes in the other.

Three miles from Cilonen, turn right, ignoring minor turning which has 'no right turn' sign. Turn left onto the B4295 and enter Llanrhidian. Ignore fingerpost pointing downhill. Turn right opposite The Greyhound in Oldwalls, for Weobley Castle, a late-medieval fortified Manor, 13th and early 14th century.

In half a mile, by village sign for Landimore, turn left and go uphill in unclassified lane. After one mile there is a sudden exit onto a main road, right on a bend as it drops sharply downhill. Turn right and continue to bottom of hill.

Just before bridge, turn left to Fairyhill. Keep straight ahead at junction in half a mile, and climb as road bears left up to Cefn Bryn common, with views over flat land below to your right. Beware of sheep.

Pass Reynoldston Post Office and shop in a dip, and the King Arthur Hotel set back on your right. Go right (not hard right) at crossroads signed Oxwich, and left at junction with the A4118. In one mile, turn right, signed to Oxwich, by some ruins and fancy wrought iron gates leading to Penrice Castle grounds (Private). The hill is 1:5 downwards. The road runs through an unspoilt environment of rushes, wildflowers and pools with water-lilies.

Arriving in Oxwich, there are shops on your right. The route turns right at the crossroads. However, to the left is the Oxwich Bay Hotel, which has a large beer garden overlooking the sea, and beyond it, at the end of the lane, St Illtyd's church is submerged in woodland, while the high tide clamours below. There are toilets on the left of the road to the pub.

Oxwich Castle is straight ahead at the crossroads, uphill, signed to Slade and a Holiday Park. It's a 16th century Tudor manor house, now ruined, and stands on private land.

Having explored all the other directions, return to the crossroads, and go towards Penrice. Pass a row of old cottages on the right. A craft shop occupies the old post office, built in 1760 and established as a shop in 1834. John Wesley 'lodged and preached' in The Nook, between 1764 – 1771. Go uphill for a mile. At the junction, turn left. Follow sign for Horton at first, but at the crossroads one mile further on, keep straight ahead and avoid going down into Horton. At crossroads with the A4118, turn right, then first left, the B4247, as you come to Scurlage. (The unsurfaced track opposite at the crossroads cuts the corner and saves almost a mile. It was due to be upgraded as a Bridle Path in August

1993. During World War 2 it was used by military vehicles but in anything other than drought conditions it's very muddy).

Continue to Rhossili, whose sweeping bay with golden sands backed by high dunes is one of the most photographed views in Wales, and is every bit as splendid as any postcard ever makes it look.

Rhossili has a Hotel, a National Trust shop, tearooms, B&Bs, Guest Houses, & ice-cream vans. You can walk out to Worms Head, a Nature Reserve area (depending on the tide). In Spring and early summer there are restrictions to avoid disturbing nesting birds. Return from Rhossili on the B4247 to Scurlage. There are shops here, including a pharmacy, and The Countryman pub.

Turn left onto the A4118. In a couple of miles, take left turn to Reynoldston. At crossroads continue uphill following sign to Llanrhidian. It's a steady pull up to the top of the moor. At the peak of the hill, there is a wide grassy track leading off the road to your left to Arthur's Stone half a mile away.

An easy run down past Broad Pool brings you to the B4271 where you turn right. Stay on this road for almost five miles, then go ahead on the A4118 where this comes in from the right.

Go through Upper Killay, past Post Office on your left, and downhill. Look for a warning triangle showing a bicycle and sign 'Civic Amenities site' on your right, on a railway bridge. Enter site by Railway Inn (if you're going on to Laugharne take track in opposite direction, behind pub) and join Clyne Valley Bike Path, constructed over disused railway line. (To shorten Gower ride and continue to Laugharne, turn down past Welcome to Town pub and on to Marsh Road. Rejoin B4295 at Crofty. Entering Gowerton, take left turn into Pont-y-Cob and follow instructions on page 64; 7mls/12km to here from Llanrhidian.) Ride for two miles down a wooded valley beside streams and a pond. This connects with the Swansea Bay to Mumbles bike path near the golf course and boating pond. Take care crossing road. Pedestrian-controlled traffic lights have been requested.

Weobley Castle, Gower

A medieval castle overlooking the marshes that border the Loughor estuary, it dates from the 13th century.

See also **Oxwich Castle,** a 16th century Tudor Manor House, and dovecote, in ruins.

Arthur's Stone (Maen Ceti)

A neolithic cairn, date about 4000 BC, give or take a thousand years. A very big stone, resting on several uprights. The source of many legends but not too many facts, its size makes it a spectacle.

Rhossili

The Church of St Mary was built about 1300 – 1350. The doorway, with fine dogtooth and chevron moulding, is earlier still, and was probably retrieved from a church on the dunes which was overwhelmed by sand. A 'scratch' sundial is marked out on the top of the left hand pillar, with a hole in the centre for a stick. The stick's shadow indicated the time.

Inside the church is a memorial to Petty Officer Edgar Evans R.N., who died with Captain Scott on the Antarctic Expedition of 1912.

Mumbles Lighthouse

14. 'A Bit Too Much of a No-Good Boyo'

Laugharne – Pendine – Laugharne

Distance: 15mls/24km.

Longer Option: Continue round coast to Manorbier.

Terrain: Easy, except for hill returning from Pendine.

Accommodation/Refreshments/Supplies: Many Guest Houses and B&Bs in Laugharne. Hotel at Pendine. All kinds of accommodation around Saundersfoot and Tenby, including camp-sites, and Youth Hostel at Pentlepoir, near Saundersfoot. Small supermarket in Laugharne and many pubs, including Browns Hotel, much frequented by Dylan Thomas in his day and by his admirers ever since. Shops, take-aways, cafés and the Beach Hotel in Pendine.

Toilets: In Laugharne and Pendine.

Rail Access: Carmarthen. 13mls/21km.

Tourist Information: At Boat House in Laugharne.

Things to see on this ride: Laugharne Castle ruins. The tidal Taff estuary which inspired much of Dylan Thomas' work. The poet's workshop, his boat house home (now a museum), his grave and his favourite drinking places. Pendine Sands, six miles of firm, flat sands once used for car racing.

How to Connect with Next Ride: From Pendine to Manorbier trying to follow the coast is a very scenic ride, but can be frustrating. A lot of energy is expended without making progress in the desired direction. Via Amroth, Wiseman's Bridge, Saundersfoot and Tenby, 29mls, 42km.

Route

Starting Point: The Cross in the Square, (The Grist), opposite the Castle.

Leave Laugharne by the back way – behind the Cross and out through Water Street with its little stream running beside it. Keep straight ahead on a not-too-exacting climb for two-thirds of a mile, then fork left. A tranquil ride on country lane for 3 miles, riding between high banks topped with hedges, so not much to see. Straight on at crossroads at Three Lords, where the most obvious feature is a huge stack of car tyres. Signs to Amroth and Red Roses.

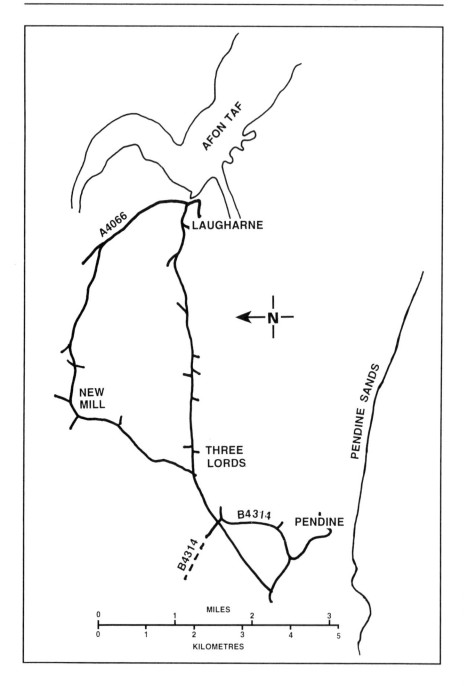

500 yards from here, to your right on a bend, a ruined Ebenezer Chapel, now used as storage space for farm implements, records that it was founded in 1862, to commemorate the 'Becentenary (sic) of the Heroes of Conscience of 1662'. The phrase has a contemporary ring, yet what tale of betrayal, torture or death is alluded to, would be hard to discover now.

Most of this part of Wales took the Royalist side in the Civil War, as is witnessed by the destruction of so many Castles by the once-victorious Cromwell. By 1662, the Monarchy had been finally restored for two years. Were these Heroes the last of a dissident minority? Faithfully honoured for two hundred years, their suffering is lost in the welter of subsequent conflicts.

Straight ahead, keeping to minor road at crossroads with the B4314. A nice run down for three quarters of a mile. Left at a T-junction for Pendine. Pass the rather grand church, and go right for the beach. A smooth wide road, down a 20% hill. There are repeated warnings to take care. The road looks as though it terminates at the sea wall but in fact it makes a tight turn to your left. A plaque commemorates a bus driver who died saving his passengers' lives here.

The main road along the coast is crowded, particularly in summer, and the seaward side is a Danger Area. It's best to go back up the hill on the B4314, turn right at crossroads into minor road where you were earlier, and retrace your wheel marks as far as the next crossroads at Three Lords.

Turn left for New Mill. This gives you a rewarding two mile descent through woods alongside a little stream, reminiscent of the woods above Tintern. In New Mill keep right, following signs to Laugharne, and right again a short way up hill. After one mile keep straight on at unmarked junction where road joins from the left. Ride a comfortable 1.5 miles.

Take heed that the road joins the A4066 abruptly and on the wrong side. Turn right for final one mile descent into Laugharne, passing St Martin's church and Dylan Thomas's burial place on your left.

Laugharne/Talacharn

Before Dylan Thomas happened to Laugharne, it was a dozy town with an 'end of the line' look. Its sister town on the next peninsular, Llanstephan, still looks that way. Dylan was 'a bit too much of a no-good boyo, he was', in the opinion of one local resident who claimed to have known him.

Laugharne's made a good thing out of her penniless poet, all the same. There are town trails and souvenir shops, the Museum and the drinking places, while the cause of it all lies in a rough grave, with no headstone, edging or ornament – only a simple, white-painted cross. Laugharne Castle has two 12th century towers, and St Martin's church is also Norman.

The Boat House Museum, Art Gallery Video/Audio display bookshop and tea room are open 10.00 am – 5.15 pm, Easter – October and weekends in winter. The tacky writing shed where Dylan Thomas actually did his writing is further along the walled walk. Steps lead down to the estuary, still visited by the sea and the priestly herons.

Pendine Sands

The Beach Hotel at Pendine was the Headquarters for attempts on the World Land Speed Record between 1924 and 1927. In those years the Record was broken five times, three times by Malcolm Campbell and twice by J.G. Parry Thomas, who died trying to even the score. A plaque at the Hotel gives details of dates and the times achieved. Cars still drive on the firm level sands.

Opposite: the clock tower in Laugharne

15. Gerald the Tireless Tourist, and the Old Man and the Rock

Manorbier – St Govans – Pembroke – Lamphey Palace – Manorbier

Distance: 28mls/45km

Longer Option: Continue to Carew for Ride 16.

Shorter Options: Returning from Bosherton without going to St Govans would save about 3.5mls/5.6km – too little to be worth the sacrifice of such a highlight. Cutting the corner from Freshwater East to Lamphey would shorten the distance drastically to about 13mls/21km. It would still be a pleasant ride with views.

Terrain: Not too hard – some cracking downhills.

Accommodation/Refreshments/Supplies: A few hotels in Pembroke, plus pubs, cafés and shops. Youth Hostel/ Camping in Manorbier. Widespread B&Bs. All facilities in Tenby. Small shops in Manorbier for picnic supplies. Pub in Bosherton.

Toilets: In Pembroke, opposite Texaco garage; in Mill Pond Walk, near car park at hill below Castle and at the Castle itself.

Rail Access: Manorbier or Tenby.

Tourist Information: Haverford West or Tenby.

Things to see on this Ride: Manorbier Castle, Bosherton Lily Ponds, St Govans Head and Chapel, Pembroke Castle, Lamphey Palace. Superlative rugged coastal scenery, cliffs and beaches. Gannets, puffins, and other sea birds. Seals and Dolphins are frequently seen.

How to Connect with Next Ride: After leaving Lamphey, ride for two miles on the Ridgeway towards Tenby. Turn left for Milton, then briefly right on the A477. Next left for Carew. 5mls/8km.

Route

Starting point: Manorbier Castle.

Leave town with the castle on your right and car park on your left. Downhill initially, then up to viewpoint over the bay. The Castle's on

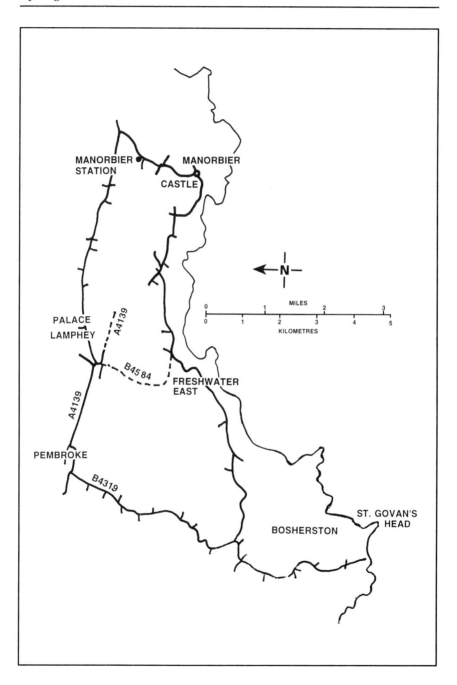

one hill, the 13th century Norman church on another. Go left at cross-roads. In one mile, briefly join the A4139 on a bend. (The major road comes in from your right). Very soon, take first left. Road is 'unsuitable for motors', but that doesn't include the ever-busy tractors. Entering Freshwater East, you pass bungalows, and the Freshwater Inn with its sea view.

(**Short ride:** Go ahead here onto the B4584 to Lamphey, where you rejoin main route).

At top of rise, turn left by BT building signed Stackpole and Traeth (beach). Check your brakes and be ready for a knickerbockerglory of a hill! It's signalled with double warnings – Hill 1:5 and Hill 15% – either way, it's a drop. Wide, smooth, gently curved and with excellent visibility, it's one to relish. There's a good long run-out at the end, but be prepared for the 'road narrows' sign – the road not only narrows drastically but simultaneously makes a tight turn over a bridge. As you finish the climb which inevitably follows, pause to look back at the coast you're leaving. Continue through East Trewent.

Ride for nearly 3 miles to junction with the B4319. Turn left for 400 yards. At junction take second left (the centre road of three roads), signed to Bosherton.

Bosherton church and the footpath to the Lily Ponds are on the left. The lily ponds are a memorable sight in their season, but the path is for walkers only. Bear right. Cafe and St Govan's pub on your left. (If you're not going to St Govan's, skip the next paragraph).

Keep to the furthest right road, and check with Notice whether the Army firing range is active. A broken cattle grid is danger enough. There's a second grid at the entrance to the car park. This is a bleak place, scoured by winds, and even in summer sun can seem austere. The whole area is pock marked with bunkers and Ministry of Defence notices.

Return through Bosherton to junction with the B4319. Turn right onto main road. The church of St Petroc can be seen from afar. St Pedroc was the uncle of St Cadoc.

The remaining few miles to Pembroke are uneventful but for Windmill Hill, 1:7 or 14%, which brings you down to the town in style. Left for Pembroke Castle (One way).

Leave Pembroke on the A4139 for Penally and Tenby, under railway bridge, where there's a small sign for Lamphey. In Lamphey, turn left on bend by church, and immediately take small lane on left to see Lamphey Palace.

From Lamphey Palace, return to top of lane and turn left onto Ridgeway road towards Tenby. Four miles from Lamphey take right turn to Manorbier Station. Go over level crossing, briefly left on the A4139, then right for Manorbier.

Manorbier Castle

Gerald of Wales was born here in 1146. He's famous for touring Wales to gather support for the Third Crusade, and writing his descriptions of the journey in fascinating and sometimes fanciful detail. His Itinerary is much used as source material by later scholars. He calls Manorbier 'the pleasantest spot in Wales' and discounts the idea that he might be prejudiced. Open daily Easter to September 10.30 to 5.30 pm.

Bosherton Lily Ponds

Those who claim that Arthur's Court was in West Wales, say the sword Excalibur was thrown into one of these lakes. The water-lilies are at their best in early summer.

St Govans Chapel

Tradition tells that in the sixth century, St Govan, pursued by pirates, crept into a fissure in the rock, which kindly widened until he was safely in and closed behind him. His Chapel gives the impression of having been shoehorned into the rock. Go along the road to the old Coast Guards' look-out, and look back at where you know the Chapel to be, to appreciate the legend of its invisibility.

Pembroke Castle

Built on a peninsular surrounded on three sides by water, Pembroke Castle is a well preserved Norman Castle, dating from 1200. It was damaged in the civil war by Cromwell's forces. Henry VII ('Harry' Tudor) was born here in 1456. Castle open all year except for Sundays between November and February, and December 25th, 26th and 1st January. Tel: 0646 681510 for information on Tours and charges.

Lamphey Palace

The arcaded parapets remind us that Lamphey shared an architect with St Davids. Queen Elizabeth the First's toyboy, the Earl of Essex, once lived here. He fell out of favour and the Palace fell to ruin.

If you have to carry your bike on a car, some cars are more suitable than others!

16. Oysters and Ale . . . and an Old Mill by a Stream

Carew Castle – Oyster Farm – Cresswell Quay – Blackpool Mill – Llawhaden Castle – Picton Castle – Oakwood Pleasure Park – Carew.

Distances: 30mls/48km; 26mls/42km; 17mls/27km; 6.5mls/10.5km

Options: This ride divides naturally into 3 parts. Returning direct from Picton instead of via Llawhaden Castle would cut out 4mls/6.5km and a hill. Returning from Blackpool Mill would reduce distance to 17mls/27km. A short circuit from Carew to Cresswell Quay and back is 6.5mls/10.5km.

Longer Option: Continue to Haverford West for next Ride.

Terrain: The shortest ride has only one moderate hill. The ride to Blackpool Mill has two or three but none are very long. The longest hill, 1.5 miles, is up to Llawhaden Castle. Apart from this one effort, it's an easy ride.

Accommodation/Refreshments/Supplies: Hotels in Haverford West. All kinds of accommodation in Tenby. Youth Hostel and camping at Manorbier. Pubs at Carew. Cafe at Blackpool Mill. Restaurant at Picton Castle. Many eateries at Oakwood.

Toilets: In Haverford West, mostly in car parks! Near Information Office, Hill Street car park and the car park behind museum.

Rail Access: Manorbier. (Sundays May – September only).

Tourist Information: In Haverford West (summer only).

Things to see on this Ride: Carew Castle, Tidal Mill, Celtic Cross. Oyster Farm. Traditional riverside pub at Cresswell Quay. Blackpool Mill. Picton Castle and Graham Sutherland Art Gallery. Llawhaden Castle. Oakwood Pleasure Park. Fascinating tidal river, wild life.

How to Connect with Next Ride: Ride 17, Haverford West. Picton Castle is 4mls/6.5km from Haverford West. Turn left where route crosses the A40, as marked in text.

Route

Starting point – Carew Castle.

From the Castle, follow the A4075 downhill, past Mill and Celtic Cross. Immediately after crossing bridge, turn left and ride beside the water, signed West Williamston. Pass picnic site on left on a bend, and go on for 1.6 miles. On the left, take a small un-surfaced lane signed to Carew Oyster farm, situated where there were once quarries.

Back at the road, keep on until you come to a telephone box, where you go straight ahead, on the middle one of three roads. Ride for a couple of miles along a pretty lane bordered with rushes, wildflowers and brambles. Up a steep but short hill. Keep left at junction where larger road joins from your right. Downhill to Cresswell Quay.

A long low building on your right, smothered in creeper and trailing plants, appears to be a private house until you catch sight of the stack of barrels by the door. Food is not served, but beer arrives on the counter in a large jug, frothing like the pictures on a Dickensian Christmas card.

Outside on the Quay, against a backdrop of deciduous woods, picnic tables overlook the water. This is a tidal creek where otters breed and wild fowl and wading birds gather in thousands. If you can arrange for a clear night and a full tide, sunset over the creek is a sight to haunt the memory.

(Shortest ride returns from here. Start back the way you came, up the hill, but keep left on main road. Pass Pisgah chapel. Go right at crossroads signed to West Williamston. Take first turning left, a small lane, to Carew Newton. Straight on when smaller lanes cross. Downhill, and left at a T-junction to emerge on bend by the picnic site. Retrace steps for last mile to Carew Castle. There's an even better view of the bridge from this direction).

Longer ride continues: Leave the pub on your right and ride uphill. Go straight ahead at crossroads where the road you're on bears left. After 1.25 miles, continue ahead, (slightly right) as road curves round to left. Blind corner here.

Avoid going into Martlewy. Keep straight on for almost two miles to Minwear. As road bends to the right, Minwear church is a short way

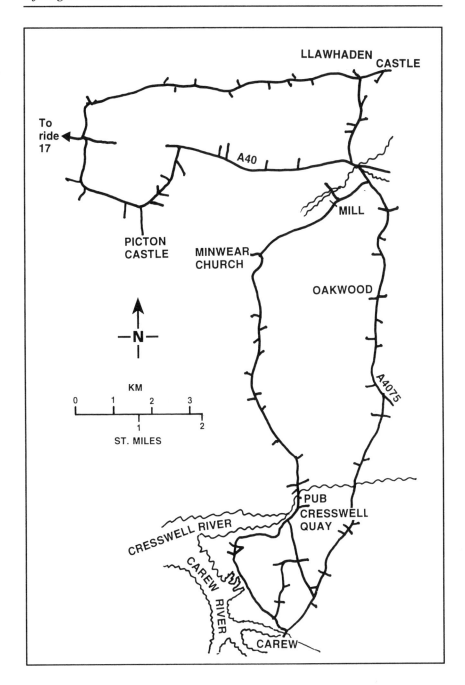

down a lane to your left. A 12th century church, connected with the Knights of Jerusalem, it turns its back to the road. The most obvious entrance, now disused, faces the open fields. The font, decorated with carvings of human heads, was retrieved from a nearby farm where it had served as a pig trough.

Regain the road and climb steeply to picnic site. Another mile brings you to Blackpool Mill. Turn left to junction with lay-by on the A4075.

(Intermediate ride, return from here on the A4075).

Turn left for Canaston bridge, and left at the T-junction with the A40. Avoiding the A40 here means a diversion and extra climbing. Better to stick with it – it's only 3 miles to left turning for Rhos and Picton Castle. Downhill for 1.5 miles. Turn left in Rhos village and it's another half mile to Picton Castle.

To omit loop to Llawhaden, ride back to Canaston Bridge and take the A4075 back to Carew.
To continue from Picton: Return to Rhos village and turn left, ride for two miles.
To continue to Haverford West for Ride 17: turn left on A40.

Cross the A40 at offset crossing, left-right, signed to Wiston. Ride along wooded lane, which changes to very high banked hedges. Keep straight on at fork, signed to Llawhaden. Pass Woodlands Farm Park. Continue into Llawhaden, stopping at Post Office on corner, set back from junction, where you can obtain leaflets and information on the Castle.

Go on down the hill. There is an information board and a picnic site just before left turn to Castle. Llawhaden Castle has sign 'Dim beiciau cwn' (No bikes/dogs). At least bikes get first mention. There's not much room for parking bikes, as the space in front of the entrance is blocked by cars struggling to turn round. Leaving the Castle, return to centre of Llawhaden village and take turning by Post office signed to the A40.

There's now a whopper downhill run for 2 miles. Turn left and almost immediately right to cross Canaston bridge and the A40. To avoid riding the same way twice, return now on the A4075, keeping on this road all the way to Carew Castle.

Oaklands Pleasure Park is 2mls/3km on your right. Although this is an 'A' road, it's not usually too busy, and it's a comfortable ride. People from outside Wales often comment on the lack of traffic there – even major roads such as the A40 go through long stretches of quiet country-side.

Carew Castle

This castle is spectacular in a way which contrasts vividly with the more usual hilltop variety. It's gracious and elegant rather than menacing. Picnic parties relax, and farm animals browse, by its natural moat.

Carew Castle (Wales Tourist Board)

Carew Celtic Cross

This Cross with its striking changes of geometric patterns, including a swastika design,is right by the road near the entrance to the Castle. A swastika was a symbol of good luck to the Celts, who saw it as representing the rays of the sun. The word itself derives from the Sanskrit and means 'well-being'. The amount of painstaking effort needed to cover a massive stone with this density of decoration, using the tools available in the 11th century, demands admiration.

Carew Oyster Farm

Here you can see illustrated the system for nurturing oysters for the 2 – 5 years it takes them to mature ready for the table. Timber trestles in the Carew river assist in increasing the flow of water over the young oysters as the high tides flood in twice a day. Sales, mail order and recipes for those who like them.

Blackpool Mill

A pleasant café, with tables on a terrace overlooking the mill stream, and on the cared-for lawns. Home-made cakes and savouries so delicious they're sure to be bad for you, but who cares? Tours of Mill available. Craft shop.

Llawhaden Castle

Gerald of Wales visited his uncle here in 1175 AD. Many battles, devastations and rebuildings have left their marks throughout the ages, but the ruins, mostly 14th century, and the moat, 70ft/21m wide and about 25ft/7.6m deep, are still impressive. The well in the courtyard is over 100ft/30.5m deep. Ensuring a water supply to last a siege was one of any Castle defender's main worries.

Picton Castle and Art Gallery

Picton Castle, a 'Stately Home', has been inhabited without a break from 1302. The Art Gallery displays a collection of paintings presented by

Graham Sutherland, (1903 – 80) who was much inspired by the Pembrokeshire countryside.

Grounds are open 1 April – 30 September, but closed on Mondays unless Bank Holiday. Tours of Castle mid-July to mid-September certain days only, but open Bank Holidays. Sutherland Gallery, check opening times. Craft shop. Garden shop.

Oakwood Pleasure Park

The largest theme park in Wales, Oakwood covers 80 acres. Open March to October.

Woodlands Farm Park

Open 10am – 6pm. Animals may be fed at any time on food costing 30p a bag. Ring 0437 731548

17. 'Ports and Happy Havens'.

Haverford West – Martin's Haven – St Brides Haven – Little Haven – Broad Haven – Nolton Haven – Haverford West.

Distance: 40 miles.

Shorter Options: Going straight to Little Haven would make the ride a more manageable 25 miles. You could return on the B4341 from Broadhaven for a really easy ride. You would still see the contrasting seascapes of Little and Broad Havens but you would miss the truly spectacular stretch of coast through Druidston.

Terrain: Hills. One or two toughies, though nothing really enormous. Winds often more of a problem.

Accommodation/Refreshments/Supplies: All you need in Haverford West. Hotels/ pubs in Littlehaven and Broadhaven. Youth Hostels at Broadhaven and Solva (near Penycwm). A great many camping sites. Holiday cottages and static caravans for rent. Shops for picnic supplies in Broadhaven. Mariners' Arms at Nolton Haven. Penry Arms at Sutton.

Toilets: Martin's Haven, St Bride's Haven, Little Haven and Haverford West (as for Ride 16)

Rail Access: Haverford West.

Tourist Information: Haverford West and Broadhaven (summer).

Things to see on this Ride: Beaches and coastal scenery. Wildlife, particularly sea-birds, and seals. Castle ruins and Museum in Haverford West.

How to Connect with Next Ride: Ride 18, St Davids. From Nolton Haven turn right immediately after crossing bridge. A hefty climb up Folkeston Hill. Left on the A487 and right at crossroads by Motel. Pass 13th century Roch Castle – it's for hire as a holiday cottage if you write to the owners. Down hill, straight on at crossroads, left at junction, and left to 'Brandy Brook'. Good road through woods, ford across small river by fixed caravan site – goodness knows how they got these great big vans down here. At the end of the road, a sign declares it Anaddas i fodur ('unfit for cars')! Up a nasty hill. Pass Eweston Farm. Go left at the fork, left at a T-junction and left immediately after the entrance to Brawdy Farm. Turn right onto the A487 at Penycwm. Take next right past RAF Brawdy, then left opposite main entrance, past caravan site. Carry on to Middle Mill and join in next ride. About 15 miles.

Route

Starting Point: Haverford West Railway Station.

Take the A4076 signed Milford Haven. At the roundabout a couple of hundred yards ahead, keep left into Freeman's Way by-pass which quickly takes you clear of the town.

At the Merlin's Bridge roundabout use the second exit signed Milford Haven and after a very short distance take right turning signed Tiers Cross. A rural road, but with a scattering of light industries and a couple of lopsided bends. In Tiers Cross, turn right after the Welcome Traveller into narrow road with the usual high banks and hedges. Softly down until an abrupt corner at Rosemoor farm. Short steep bit down, left at junction and left again at 'Give Way'. Climb up past the grandly situated but isolated church on your left, then descend again through woodland, with quarry on your right. Up the other side, round a rabble of bends to an open plateau where sheep are the main occupiers. An acute corner by Capeston farm, then continue to Hasguard Cross crossroads. If you're taking the shorter ride, go straight across here. Resume at 'Little Haven'.

For a longer ride, turn left on the B4327. A rather plain road at first, with an unaggressive dip-and-up across a stream. Go ahead at crossroads, signed St Brides, where the B4327 turns left for Dale and Marloes. Take first turning left, down a twisty country road. Not much view thanks to the hedges, but interesting gnarled ancient trees, and several ruined cottages and abandoned stone walls. Try not to ride past Lower Hoaten Farm behind the cows!

A bit further on, Pearsons is a large rather grand farmhouse with impressive gates. Left at crossroads with dead-end straight ahead. (You come back to this point later). Return to the B4327. Turn right, cross bridge and turn right very soon after, for Marloes. There are two pubs in quick succession in Marloes, the Foxes Inn, which does B & B, and the Lobster Pot Inn. Pass the clock tower, Post office/store and small village green.

The ride down the tip of the peninsular is a super ride on a rolling road with non-strenuous ups and pleasant downs. You look across farms to jagged cliffs and rocks, with the shape of the land plain to see, until the precipitous drop to the beach at Martin's Haven. The last few hundred yards are rough and too steep to ride comfortably. The tiny,

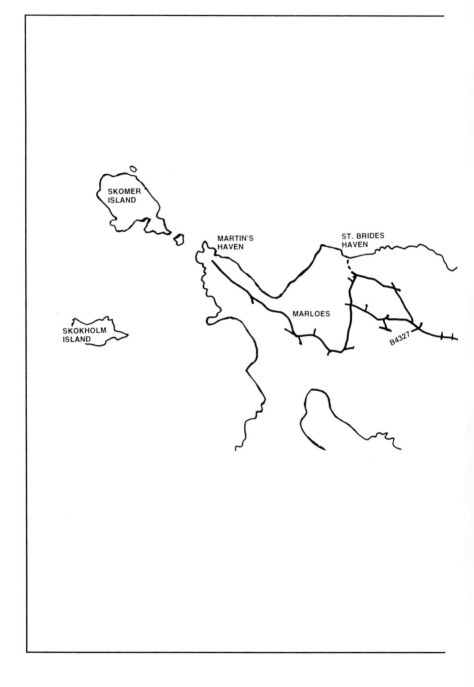

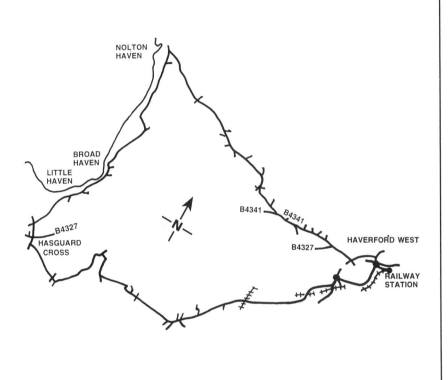

stony beach is used by fishermen and divers, and by the Dale Princess to-ing and fro-ing to the islands of Skomer, Skokholm and Grassholm.

Retrace your wheel spins through Marloes, left at the B4327, over bridge, left to cross roads with dead-end road where you were earlier. Now continue straight ahead. At junction take small road to left signed 'Traeth' (Beach), down to St Brides Haven. A little green with a solitary farm and a church 'at the sea-down's edge between wind-ward and lee'. The church is kept locked. The Coast Path goes through the churchyard, where there are some eye-catching but modern Celtic Crosses. Views over grassland to 'Castle', now a Property Bond Home. The beach is rocky and seals can be seen close inshore. There are toilets (locked out of season).

Up to the road again, continue on straight road. Pass remnants of Talbenny airfield, once an anti-submarine base used by 311 (Czech) Squadron, partnered by 304 (Polish) Squadron at Dale, but deserted since 1946.

At the crossroads go ahead on the B4327 as far as Hasguard Cross, where you now turn left, signed Little Haven. Take the first turn right, down a brisk hill. An ornamental pond is the happy paddling ground of a number of ducks.

Just after the turning from Dale comes in from the left, and before hitting the hill, pause at the view point on your left-hand side. The colours depend on when you're here, but the cliffs are clothed in bracken, gorse and heather, with tiny chunks of arable inserted here and there. The hill down to Little Haven has a 30 mph speed limit which you really have to work at. It's a picturesque little place, with a teeny but perfectly formed cove. Out of season it's delightful. Toilets in car park.

Leave Little Haven by a hill that makes a backward-facing left turn, signed Broadhaven. It's a cruel gradient, but it's up-and-over – next minute you're haring down into Broadhaven.

The beach at Broadhaven is a wide curve, with lots of golden sands, unless the tide's right up. Choice of pubs/cafés/shops here. Information office in summer, in car park near Youth Hostel.

The road up from the beach climbs for one mile, running parallel to the Coast Path. Pass the quaintly-named St Madoc of Ferns Church on your right, then turn left for Druidstone. Cattle grid here. A beautiful coastal ride through the Pembrokeshire National Park, with views of sea and rocks. It's a switchback ride of swoops and climbs. The hills are not long but they're fierce. When you reach the top of a hill and look back, you'll appreciate why it is you're out of breath. 'Pembrokeshire's puffing country', as one local cyclist put it.

After about 4mls/6.4km, you come to a junction with a Chapel on your left and the Mariners' Arms opposite. Turn down to the left to the beach at Nolton Haven. This small bay is almost exactly in the centre of St Brides Bay. It's shut in behind rocky cliffs on either side. A notice board explains the requirements for testing the quality of bathing water according to EEC standards. Nolton Haven and Broadhaven both have excellent water quality. (Leave Ride here to join Ride 18.)

Nolton Haven chapel

To return, go back uphill with the Mariners' Arms on your left and Chapel on your right. Climb ahead through woods for half a mile to Nolton. Bear left at junction. Pass St Madoc's Parish church on your left.

Ride through the village, climbing more gently for next half mile. Straight on at Nolton crossroads, signed Pelcomb. This is a lovely road. Sometimes the view's hidden by hedges, but there are more open places. Keep straight ahead at unsigned junction, on narrow road with views of rolling farmland, and straight on at junction signed Haverford West. Down into Sutton, keeping left at junction, following signs to Haverford West. Penry Arms on your left. This pub is on my personal short-list of first rate pubs. Real Ales, sandwiches with twice as much filling as sandwich, and everywhere polished and shiny. You can afford to linger, it's only 2.5mls/4km to Haverford West on the B4341, and it's downhill all the way.

Haverford West

Haverford West is a spider's web with 11 roads feeding in to it from every direction. The ruined Castle on the hill was 'slighted' by Cromwell, in spite of having surrendered. The town was burnt by both Llewellyn the Great and Owain Glyndŵr and its function as a Port was taken over by Milford Haven.

St Mary's 13th century church has some interesting features. Amongst the carvings on the capitals of the nave arcades is one of a pig playing a 'crwth' or fiddle – a variation on the cat and the fiddle idea, perhaps. Quakers from Haverford West founded Haverford County in Pennsylvania USA. Ornate Early Victorian iron balconies can still be seen on some buildings – a style of decoration exported around the world.

18. A Capital Circuit
St David's/Tyddewi

Distance: 16.5mls/26.5km

Longer Option: Carry on to Fishguard.

Terrain: A gentle ride with lots of flat bits, but a couple of short hills and one long one up to Whitchurch.

Accommodation/Refreshments/Supplies: Hotels, Guest Houses, B&Bs in St David's. Youth Hostel and camping at Whitesands. Cafes, Pubs and shops in St David's. Youth Hostels at Trevine, and Pwll Deri, near Strumble.

Toilets: In car park at Whitesands Bay.

Rail Access: Fishguard 16mls/26km N. Haverford West 15mls/24km E.

Tourist Information: St Davids.

Things to see on this Ride: St David's, smallest city in Britain. Cathedral, Bishop's Palace. Splendid coastal scenery and the most westerly point in Wales. Possibilities of seeing grey seals. Attractive fishing harbour at Porth-Clais. Middle Mill – a curious village which deserves to be a tourist attraction, but thankfully isn't.

How to Connect to Next Ride: The A487 goes direct from St David's to Goodwick, and is not particularly busy but the road nearest the coast is prettier. Trevine/Trefin and Abercastle are picturesque villages, worth a look. Leaving Abercastle, you have to retreat inland. Turn left at crossroads and thread your way northwards. Join circuit of Strumble Head as described in Ride 19. (Page 104, from Lighthouse.)

Route

Starting Point: Cross Square, St Davids.

Take the Porth-Clais road, dropping down after one mile to the small boat harbour. Cross the stream, go round past the car park and up the hill, enjoying views of the sea and of the solid bulk of Carn Llidi ahead. Straight on at the crossroads. At the T-junction, you may like to go left for about a mile to see the Lifeboat station at St Justinians, and have a sight of Ramsey island. Return to this point.

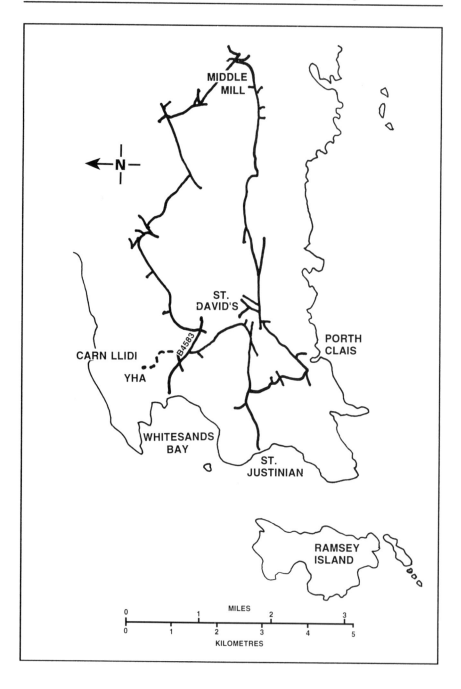

Back towards St David's, go left at fork, uphill and on a bend just as the Cathedral comes into view through sheltering line of trees. Climb left for Whitesands Bay, riding down a narrow road between high banks, with the mountain ahead. Turn left to go down to beach.

Whitesands is another picture postcard beach, from which, it's said, St Patrick set out for Ireland. Much depends on the time of year how agreeable you find it – that vast car park is there for a reason, but the sands are big enough to disperse everyone and still appear uncrowded. In summer there are ice-cream vans. There are toilets here, and advice on what to do with a stray seal pup if you find one – leave it alone!

Back up the hill, following the B4583. Pass the left turn which leads to the Youth Hostel, and take the next one left, which is unsigned. Follow road round many twists. It's flat going across the common, before once more being blinkered by hedges.

Joining a bigger road, turn left then immediately right, into what appears to be a farm track, bounded by a stone wall with a gate, usually open. The road can be seen romping off to the horizon with just one cottage on the left.

At the A487 go left. In a little under a mile, turn right to Caerfarchell where road makes a crossroads with a farm track to the left. Just beyond the village go left for Middle Mill, when road forks. Ride above a deep gully, with stream right at the bottom, and down into Middle Mill. Turn right, almost a U-turn, to climb up other side of hill for 0.75 miles, to Whitchurch. Pass Chapel and go straight ahead to ride beside disused airfield. St Davids was the home of an anti-U-boat squadron in World War 2, and Brawdy was its satellite field. However, the roles were soon reversed as Brawdy had longer and better aligned runways.

When road makes a strong curve to left, with Ministry of Defence notices on your right, keep straight on into minor road. At fork at bottom of hill, keep left and level. Enter St Davids past new housing development and County School on your right. Turn right for town centre.

St Davids

St David died around the year 600 AD. He founded a monastery and settlement in the sheltered valley just beyond reach of the sea. The monks led a life ruled by work and study. They ate little but bread and vegetables and drank only water. The Normans took over the site and built the Cathedral in the 1178 AD. St David became patron Saint of Wales at this time. Two pilgrimages to St Davids were acknowledged as having the same spiritual value as one to Rome, a scale likely to have under-rated the difficulties of travel in Wales. It's noticeable that the floor of the Cathedral is not flat, but slopes upward to the altar. The misericords beneath the hinged seats of the stalls are elaborately carved. The Bishop's Palace was built by Bishop Gower who was also responsible for the Palace at Lamphey. The arcaded parapets were his trademark.

Opposite: St David's Cathedral (Wales Tourist Board)

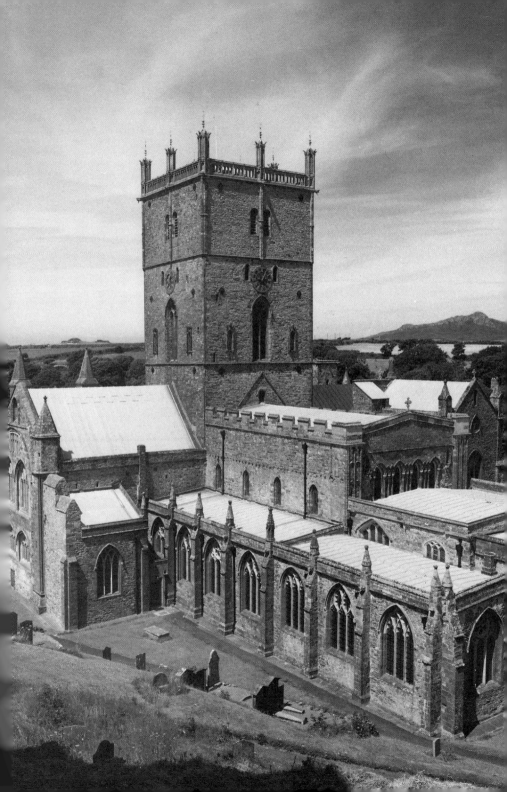

19. Round the Corner

Fishguard/Abergwaun and Strumble Head

Distance: 13.5mls/22km

Options: This ride and the next can both be fitted comfortably into one day.

Terrain: Hills.

Accommodation/Refreshments/Supplies: B&Bs galore in Fishguard, for people waiting for the Irish ferry. Several hotels. Youth Hostel at Pwll Deri. Good pubs in Fishguard, also shops, and small supermarket. It's only a short ride, so you can stock up before you go, and be back in time for a meal.

Toilets: Part-way up hill into Fishguard from main harbour, and near junction of West Street/Main Street.

Rail Access: Fishguard.

Tourist Information: Fishguard, corner of Main Street and Hamilton Street.

Things to see on this Ride: Fishguard Main Harbour with mile-long breakwater. (Irish Ferry sailings). Royal Oak Pub. (Story of the last invasion of Britain). Garn Fawr hill fort. Strumble Head cliffs and Light House. Wild seas.

How to Connect with Next Ride: Next ride begins in Fishguard.

Route

Starting Point: Fishguard Main Square. (With cannon).

With the Royal Oak on your right and Abergwaun Hotel on your left, ride down to the main harbour. A plaque on the promenade commemorates the attempted French invasion of 1789.

Then, with the Ferry Terminal to your right, take the road signed Goodwick from the big roundabout, up a steep hill, called 'Stop and Call' Hill. As you turn hard left with pub on the corner, there is a memorial on the wall opposite recording the vessels and lives saved by the Fishguard Life Boat, over many years. This is a vertical challenge of a hill, with superlative views down over town and harbour as its reward.

Still going uphill, the road makes a sharp bend to the right. Take next

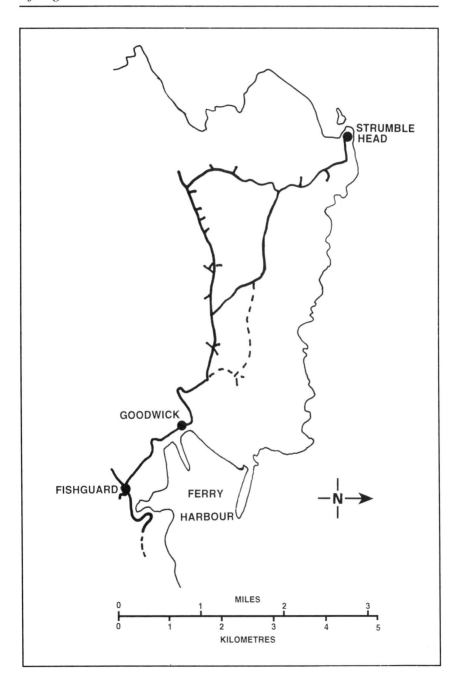

turning left, signed Strumble. Straight on at offset crossroads with telephone on right, signed Strumble.

An easy section now, riding below the crests for 2.5 miles. Pass five or six farm tracks to the right. I lose count – probably you will too. Take the first road to the right, which has a T sign and appears to head straight for Garn Fawr, a massive mound of volcanic lava garnished with an ancient hill fort. A strenuous but short pull up. As you come over the summit, views of the sea and Strumble Head light house ahead, and a good downhill run without too many bends.

Go left at the bottom to visit the lighthouse, all downhill for over a mile. The road to the lighthouse car park is busy, as people come and go, so you can find yourself sandwiched.

Returning to Fishguard, after a couple of miles there's a left turn marked 'Unsuitable for motors'. Unless it's been exceptionally dry weather, I think it's unsuitable, full stop, due to heavy use by cows, but it becomes tarmac beyond the farm. Otherwise, carry on and turn left on bigger road, to speed downhill to the Goodwick roundabout. Fishguard town centre is a mile further on, up hill, of course.

Fishguard/Abergwaun

Fishguard is known as the railway terminus for the Irish ferry. In more leisurely times, it was also used by liners going to America. The last attempted foreign invasion of Britain occurred when a French contingent came ashore at Carregwastad Point on Strumble Head, on 22nd February 1797. From all accounts they were a rag-tag-and-bobtail crew of mercenaries and desperadoes who hoped to make common cause with the Welsh against the English. They were disheartened by the sight, through the February gloom, of what they took to be a large force of redcoats coming for them. The story goes that this force consisted of women wearing red shawls and traditional black Welsh hats. The invaders surrendered and the table on which their capitulation treaty was signed can be seen in the Royal Oak public house, along with many other artefacts and photographs. A local farmer owns a grandfather clock with a bullet, aimed at Lord Cawdor, Commander of the Fishguard Fencibles, lodged in it.

The Royal Oak also has a recipe for Fishguard Pie, a tasty offering of fresh cod, leeks and mushrooms.

Strumble Head

The Light House is on an island. There is a bridge, but no access for the public. There are fine views from the cliffs in any case. As well as assisting shipping, Strumble is an important location for aircraft, being situated where two airways intersect. The R14 routes planes to Dublin, and G1 takes them to Shannon, on course for the U.S.A.

Fishguard (Wales Tourist Board)

20. The Hidden Valley

Fishguard/Abergwaun – Cwm Gwaun – Pwllgwaelod – Fishguard

Distance: 15.75mls/25km.

Longer Option: This ride can easily be joined to Fishguard/Strumble ride to give a day's riding pivoting around Fishguard.

Shorter Option: Not going to the beach at Pwllgwaelod cuts distance to 14.5mls/23km.

Terrain: One serious challenge.

Accommodation/Refreshments/Supplies: Accommodation given in previous ride. Plan to eat before or after ride.

Toilets: Head for the Hills!

Rail Access: Fishguard.

Things to see on this ride: Fishguard, see Ride 19. Secluded valley. Welsh 'Local'. Coastal views.

Tourist Information: Fishguard, corner Main Street/Hamilton Street.

How to Connect with Next Ride: There are two ways to reach Cilgerran, and both offer superlative riding. You can leave the Gwaun valley by crossing the river at Bessie's, and climbing hard up to the B4329, which will take you over the top of Mynydd Preseli, a wide-open mountain road and a lovely run on a clear day.

Or you can ride right through the Gwaun valley, and have the bonus of seeing the spectacular Pentre Ifan prehistoric megalith. The inner circle at Stonehenge was built of similar stones, from the Preseli Hills.

At the end of the valley, keep ahead, signed Maenclochog. At a T-junction near head of very steep climb, go right. (No sign the way you're going but left is to Nevern). Left at minor road, sign for Brynberian, and left at minor crossroads signed Siambr Gladdu Pentre Ifan (Burial Chamber). Follow these signs. The colossal Neolithic tomb is a short distance from the road. Return to last crossroads, go left and join the B4329 at Crosswell.

Both routes continue through Eglwyswrw, right towards Boncath on the B4332, second left for Cilgerran. 29mls/46km.

Route

Starting Point: Fishguard Main Square.

Ride down Main Street and turn right into Hamilton Street, passing Information Office on your right.

Follow the B4313 signed to Gwaun Valley and ride for 2mls/3km, before a very steep descent into Llanychaer, with bridge on your left and pub on your right. Careful as you hurtle through, people do live here. You won't keep your speed for long – a climb begins straight from the village.

The Gwaun Valley

Look out for sign to Gwaun Valley and Pontfaen as road whisks suddenly right. You carry on, over the top, into a narrow road, diving straight for the river. The Gwaun Valley is a fascinating valley, tightly wedged between wooded hills and a small active river. It's full of birdsong and lush with flowers in the meadows along the river banks.

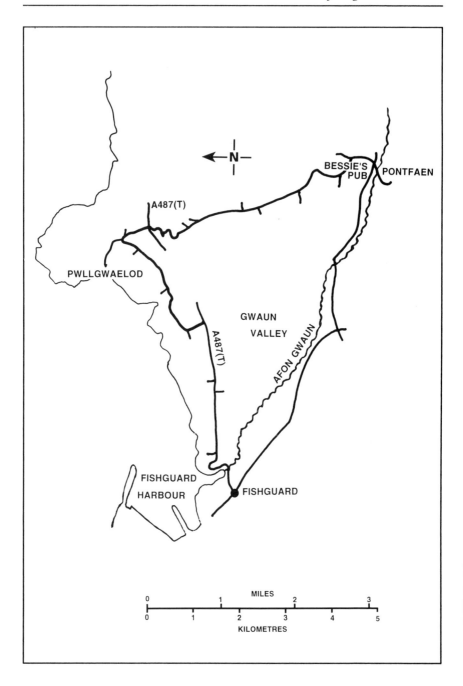

The road keeps close to the river. After almost 3 miles, you come to crossroads, with a bridge on your right and The Dyffryn Arms, known to all as 'Bessie's', on your left. 'Bessie's' has always been there. It's part of the valley, for her family have kept it since it was opened in the 1840s. Beer is served from a brimming jug.

Take the road behind the Dyffryn Arms to start a climb of 885ft/270m over two miles. Take heart, the first bit's the worst! Go left, after 0.4 miles, past a farm, easing off temporarily, then turning back to the hill.

At the summit, you ride across rock strewn open moorland, studded with gorse and heather. You have what amounts to an aerial view of both the headlands, to either side of Newport Bay. The hill down is 1 in 6 and lasts for 1.5 miles, but never mind the gradient – watch the bends! Spectacular overviews of Fishguard harbour, with a dinky-sized ferry-boat if you're lucky.

Join the A487 after a last twirl of a tight corner and an extra steep flourish. This is a traffic-infested road, but all you want to do is 50 yards, right then left, signed to Brynhenllan. At a T-junction, decide whether or not to go down to the beach at Pwllgwaelod and face the climb back. It's a lovely little beach, especially when the tide's right in. Pub down there, and toilets.

If you don't want the beach, turn left, and left again to avoid the main road for as long as possible. Pass Aber Bach. Eventually you must rejoin the A487, turning right for Fishguard. An easy 3 miles, ending in a 1:12 downhill, but mind out, the road narrows suddenly at the bottom. Pass the old harbour, used by small boats and yachts, where the Afon Gwaun meets the sea. A colourful scene before a final heave, up to the town centre.

21. Castles and Coracles

Newcastle Emlyn – Cenarth Falls – Cilgerran Castle – Newcastle Emlyn

Distance: 24.5mls/40km

Longer Option: Including a visit to Cardigan would add about 7mls/11km. Riding out to Poppit Sands and back would be another 6mls/9.6km.

Shorter Option: Visiting Cenarth Falls only would be 9mls/14.4km

Terrain: Hilly

Accommodation/Refreshments/Supplies: Very limited accommodation. There are a few possibilities in Cardigan and a Youth Hostel at Poppit Sands, 2 miles N-W of Cardigan. I know of only one Guest House in Newcastle Emlyn and one in Cilgerran. Some B&Bs around Cenarth. Shops and pubs in Newcastle Emlyn (real ale at The Pelican). Pub, café and post office/shop in Cenarth. Pubs and 'chippy' near Castle in Cilgerran.

Toilets: By cattle market in Newcastle Emlyn. River Terrace and Castle in Cilgerran.

Rail Access: 'There's no services up that way' (Quote from BR). Nearest Carmarthen, 25mls/40km.

Tourist Information: In Newcastle Emlyn (summer).

Things to see on this Ride: Newcastle Emlyn – market and Castle. Cenarth – waterfalls. Cilgerran – Castle.

How to Connect with Next Ride: From Newcastle Emlyn, the B4333 follows a pretty route to Carmarthen, winding through woods. A less dramatic ride than the Wye Valley, but also less busy. It finally joins the A484 for a five mile romp beside Afon Gwili, on its way to swell the Tywi at Carmarthen. 17mls/27km.

Route

Starting Point: Newcastle Emlyn Cattle Market.

Turn left down main street and keep left, crossing river Teifi and turning left to join the B4333, signed Aberporth.

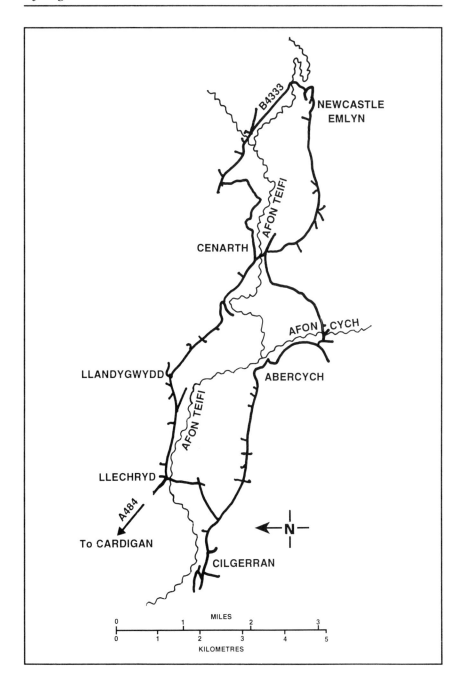

Ride beside river to Cwm Cou. Left at fork, onto the B4570. Pass an old milestone, showing 8 miles to Cardigan. Just over two miles from the start, go left part way up a hill, opposite a row of cottages, signed to Penwenallt Farm. Ride downhill. When you're sure you're about to crash through the farmer's drawing room window, the road jinks to the right and dodges briskly down the hill. As you toil up the other side, you can see back across the valley to the road you descended and the now toy-sized farmhouse.

Down again, with prudence, as it steepens before ending in junction with the A484 at Cenarth. Turn left to cross Teifi bridge and see Cenarth Falls but return to this point. (**Short Ride** – cut to last paragraph.)

Take the A484 in the direction of Cardigan for a mile and a bit. When road and river make a wide bow, take a small lane which strikes up into the woods on your right. After an initial steep climb, the lane continues parallel to the general direction of the main road. Ride to Llandygwdd. Left at junction, past Post Office, and down to rejoin the A484. Turn right for Llechryd. Left over bridge, following signs for Cilgerran. Up a hill, turn right after half a mile. Right again after another half mile to reach Cilgerran.

The way to the river terrace picnic site, half a mile below, is on your right as you come into the town. It's very scenic and peaceful by the river, with a superb view of the Castle. To see the Castle and church, climb back to the road and go on to the end of the High Street.

Return through the town, keeping straight on past the turning where you came in earlier, and straight ahead at cross roads signed Abercych. After a climb of 2.5 miles from Cilgerran, it's 1.5 miles down to the bridge at Abercych. The road jigs its way past farms and a long drawn-out village until it meets the B4332 on a sweeping bend. Turn left for a very brief drop, followed by a climb, and then a long glide all the way to Cenarth.

Turn right by the Post Office in Cenarth, following the A484 in direction of Newcastle Emlyn. In a quarter of a mile, as hill begins, turn right into small road with large farmhouse on the corner. An unkind hill for a mile, up to a crossroads with good views over town and an old fashioned finger post.

Opposite: Cenarth Falls (Wales Tourist Board)

Start down gently but then more urgently as Newcastle Emlyn and its castle come into view below. At main road turn right, then immediately left, to find yourself back in the cattle market at Newcastle Emlyn.

Newcastle Emlyn

A self-contained market town with an air of knowing its business and getting on with it. The Castle ruins stand in a strategic spot, but little is left to admire. It was yet another of the lovely castles wrecked by Cromwell for being attached to the losing side in the Civil War.

Cenarth

The waterfalls so close to the road put Cenarth on many a tourist's itinerary. 'Coracles', primitive one-man rowing boats made of wicker-work and tarred canvas, are traditionally used here for salmon fishing, but the only ones I've seen have been in museums. They look extremely hazardous but were apparently very efficient.

Cilgerran Castle

A 13th century Norman castle, Cilgerran was fought over by the Normans and the natives for a few hundred years, but it avoided involvement in the Civil War.

22. 'Here and there a grayling'

Carmarthen – Afon Cothi – Pont Ynyswen – Abergorlech – Nantgaredig – Carmarthen

Distance: 39mls/63km

Longer Option: Including the next ride to Gelli Aur would add up to 61.5mls/99km.

Shorter Options: Returning from Brechfa reduces distance to 31.5mls/51km. If you can arrange to start riding from Pont-ar-gothi, you will include the prettiest parts of the ride and reduce distances to 16.5mls/26.5km or 24mls/39km. Using the flatter B4310 saves energy – it's a pleasant road, not too busy.

Terrain: Not a hard ride, though the whole distance is perhaps better suited to Club riders rather than families. The early part of the ride is softly undulating. Moderate to fairly hard hill from Brechfa. The shorter options avoid the hill leaving Abergorlech, which is quite a toughie.

Accommodation/Refreshments/Supplies: Hotel accommodation available in Carmarthen, but not a large choice. B and B's in surrounding villages. Hotel at Pont-ar-gothi and B & B at Cothi House (Highly recommended). Excellent Pubs with (some) accommodation at Brechfa and Abergorlech. Good shops in Carmarthen. Post Office/shops at Nantgaredig, Brechfa, and Abergorlech.

Toilets: In Abergorlech.

Rail Access: Carmarthen.

Tourist Information: Carmarthen.

Things to see on this Ride: Carmarthen, the oldest town in Wales. The River Cothi (salmon river). Brecha forest. Real Ale pubs.

How to Connect with Next Ride: From Nantgaredig, cross river (B4310) and turn left on the B4300 to pick up route of next ride on far side of Llanarthney. 4mls/6.4km.

Route

Starting Point: Carmarthen Railway Station.

Turn right at end of road leading from the station and, in 100 yards, turn

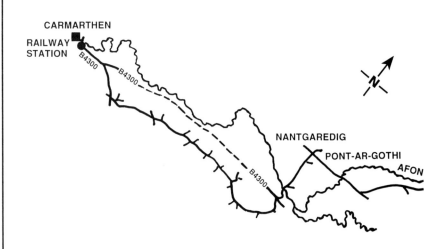

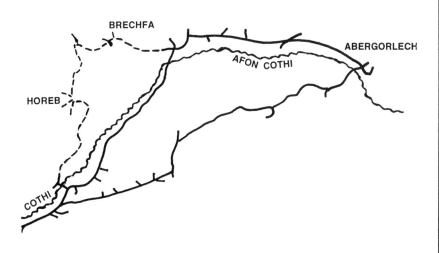

BRECHFA

ABERGORLECH

AFON COTHI

HOREB

COTHI

MILES
0   1   2   3
0   1   2   3   4   5
KILOMETRES

left at roundabout onto the B4300. After half a mile, keep straight on when the B4300 turns left. Pass Police HQ on left, climb gradually for one mile. Near top of hill, turn left into unsigned lane at off-set crossroads, opposite farm and Login Cottage.

A delightful road squirms its way between the hills for 3.5 miles. Go right at a T-junction, signed Llanddarog. In half a mile first left, just beyond a Chapel, signed Nantgaredig.

Left again, downhill, at next T-junction. The building on your right just before you arrive at the 'Give Way' sign for the B4310, is Y Polyn pub. Positioned on the corner, this pub was formerly a Toll House and featured in the Rebecca Riots of 1843.

Go left onto the B4310, then in 200 yards go right, onto the B4300, and left again to cross river – in effect an offset cross-roads. You're now back on the B4310.

In Nantgaredig, turn right briefly onto the A40 and cross Afon Cothi at Pont-ar-gothi. As you cross the bridge, the Cothi Bridge Hotel is on your right, the Cressally Arms tucked down by the water on your left, and the friendly 'local', The Salutation Arms, just ahead, in this very well-provided village. Double Dragon Real Ale from local Independent brewery Felinfoel on offer at 'the Sally'.

In 0.75 miles from the bridge, turn left, signed to Llanfynydd. After about a mile, the river Cothi appears below you through a screen of trees. Clear, clean and fast flowing, with a stony bed and sudden deeps and shallows, this little river must be twin to the one which inspired Tennyson's poem 'The Brook'.

Ride for 1.25 miles. Follow close by the river, turning left into very minor road as a climb begins. This is a single track road. Local people have said to me 'surely you don't ride that road on a bicycle, I'm scared to drive it in a car'. Happily, very few cars do use it. It would be a terrible waste, to be shut up in a vehicle. The river, buried under trees well below the road, would be invisible, and its soothing gurgle would go unheard. Look carefully and you'll spot where anglers have made tracks down to the river bank. The Cothi is known as a salmon river. I'm told fishing permits are sold at a high price. Take care in wet weather when the road is slippery – in some places it overhangs the river. A FAST BEND MAY BE YOUR LAST BEND! In misty conditions it's not always easy to be sure where the edge comes. Some sections are marked at intervals by white posts, but I think they were positioned with drivers rather than cyclists in mind.

In another half mile, there is a bridge on your left, Pont Ynyswen, with a few houses and a telephone box on the other side. Don't cross, keep on the way you're going.

The road dips and swings as the river approaches and backs away. For next five miles, you ride into a closed, heavily wooded valley, crossing little streams, occasionally passing a farm. With a final goodbye bend, the road crosses a bridge and abruptly turns its back on the river. Half a mile to T-junction with the B4310.

Shorter ride: Turn left here, through Brechfa, where you find a pretty rural Inn, The Forest Arms, and a post office/shop.

The road cuts through the side of the hill and skirts the edge of Brechfa forest. After two miles of steady climbing, turn left at crossroads in Horeb, signed to Pont Ynyswen. A short rise, then the road turns and you go straight down for two and a half miles. Steady! Cross the bridge at Pont Ynyswen, and retrace your route back through Pont ar Gothi and Nantgaredig (next Ride, see p. 115)

Turn off the A40 and cross Afon Tywi on the B4310. Turn right onto the B4300 and remain on this road for five miles. It's a pleasant easy road following the valley, with the river glimpsed at times through the trees. Return to Carmarthen on the road by which you left.

To Continue longer ride:

Turn right on the B4310 and ride four miles to Abergorlech. There's a picturesque pub, Llew Du (Black Lion) here, in a village straight from Heidi-land. Also Post office/shop, public toilets by the bridge, picnic site overlooking stream on your left on far side of town.

Cross the bridge and climb steeply for two miles, then more gently for another mile. This is the longest hill of the ride. Going up you have more time to look at the landscape – it's barely changed since the Romans were here. Woods and fields, and very few traces of human existence. Only the wind and the birdsong to listen to – until the jets go over.

Keep right and follow signs for Llanfynydd when road forks. Descend for a mile and a half, still keeping to the right, and enter a very steep narrow valley, almost a ravine. Careful – there's no room to pass a field-mouse here. Once, in full plummet, I came to what a Canadian acquaintance calls 'a serious confrontation' with an enormous furniture removal van. It was the last thing I expected to see on such a road, and almost the last thing I did see! When you reach Llanfynydd, keep to the right at the junction above the church, sign posted to Nantgaredig. Pass the back of Pant Glas Hall and rejoin road which takes you back to Pont-ar-gothi and Nantgaredig. From here follow the route given for the short ride.

Carmarthen

Carmarthen has a good claim to being the oldest town in Wales. The Romans were here – it was probably the farthest west of their settlements. The town was given a Royal Charter by King John (he of the Magna Carta) in 1201.

It possesses the remnants of a 14th century castle, a Roman fort and Ampitheatre, a 12th century church (St Peter's), the Guild-hall, 1770, a busy market, and the Bishop's Palace Museum at Abergwili. (2.3 miles from the railway station). The wizard Merlin is said to have been born here circa 480 AD.

23. The Golden Grove – a gem of a country park

Gelli Aur – Paxton's Tower – Dryslwyn Castle – Gelli Aur

Distance: 14.5mls/24km.

Longer Option: Combine with Ride 24.

Terrain: An easy ride. No long hills. A couple of slight pushes.

Accommodation/Refreshments/Supplies: Hotel, Guest House, pub with B & B and self catering accommodation in Llandeilo, but not a lot of choice. Cafe at Gelli Aur, and shop for chocolate, crisps, ice cream.

Toilets: At Gelli Aur and Castell Dryslwyn.

Rail Access: Llandeilo (4mls/6.5km) Central Wales Line, connects with Swansea.

Tourist Information: At Gelli Aur. Information Centre in town centre car park, Llandeilo is run on a voluntary basis. Further information from Dinefwr Borough Council, Tel: 0558 822521 Ext. 268.

Things to see on this Ride: Gelli Aur Country Park. Paxton's Tower. Dryslwyn Castle, River Tywi.

How to Connect with Next Ride: Turn left onto the B4300 shortly before reaching Gelli Aur and ride 4mls/6.4km to Llandeilo, to connect with next ride.

Route

Turn left from the end of Park drive, then take first right near top of hill. Signs warn of tractors crossing – treat this seriously. Right at a T-junction on blind corner, the B4297. In half a mile, on brow of hill, turn left into narrow road. Remember the tractors! A good stretch of down-hill, with views over the valley. A 'Trig' point can be seen to your right, marking the summit of Pen Pâl, 202m/656ft. You won't have time for more than a quick glimpse now, there are bends to reckon with, but in a minute you arrive at Paxton's Tower. It's worth interrupting your run to climb the Tower and admire the panorama at leisure.

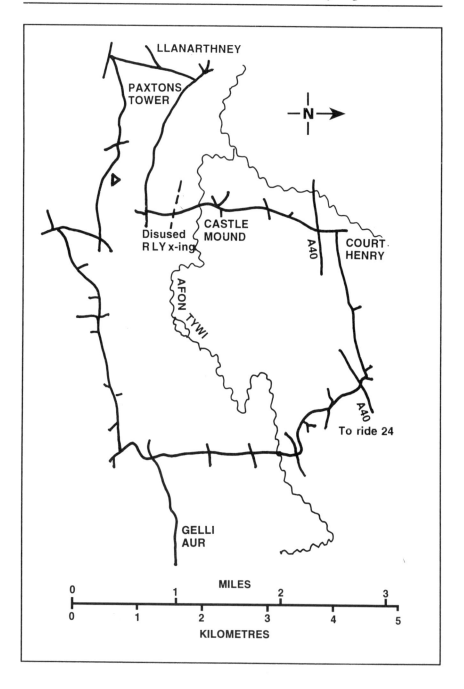

Continue downhill, sharp right at junction, down again and right at the bottom into Llanarthney. Pub opposite, church to left. Turn right, and look back at Paxton's Tower above. In 1.5 miles, turn left onto the B4297. There are some attractive stone cottages on the left, now converted into holiday homes. Cross a dismantled railway with rusty level crossing gates – once the Gorsaf Dryslwyn, constructed in 1864 and closed a year short of its centenary.

As you cross the river Tywi with its cruising swans, you see in close-up the view you had from Paxton's Tower, and can appreciate the size of the Iron Age Mound on which Castell Dryslwyn was built. Toilets in car park of picnic site on your left.

In one mile, cross the A40 into minor road signed Court Henry, and in 200 yards turn right opposite Post Office. Turn right again at a T-junction, re-cross A40. Go straight ahead at offset crossroads, signed Gelli Aur.

Part-way up the hill, a stone fountain has the inscription 'Drink and be Thankful' – but no need to be so desperate, this is the last hill which completes the square and brings you back to the country park.

Gelli Aur (The Golden Grove) Country Park

Opened by David Bellamy in August 1988, Gelli Aur offers a park-full of tame deer, peacocks, an Arboretum, and Nature Trails. The imposing Mansion (restricted access) is set in 90 acres of woodland and gardens, where five varieties of orchid can be found. It was visited by Cromwell in 1645. For once the only casualty was the deer he had for supper. It's a well-kept, hospitable place, where signs say 'Visitors are welcome to walk in our woods'. Cafeteria serves substantial snacks, and traditional Sunday lunches. Cafe terrace projects over the park, and the deer assemble below in the hope of tit-bits – they'll eat almost anything, but show a strong preference for chips with tomato sauce.

Visitor Centre with tourist information. Ice-cream and chocolate for sale. Toilets. No purpose built bicycle racks. Open all year except Christmas and Boxing Days. 10am – 7pm, April to September, otherwise 10am – 5pm. Tel: 0558 668885.

Paxton's Tower

On a fine grassy site, it commemorates Nelson's victory at the battle of Trafalgar. (Battle 1805, tower 1811). The story goes that Sir William Paxton promised to provide a bridge over the Tywi if local people supported his bid to become MP for Carmarthen. When he failed to get elected, it's alleged he took revenge by building the Tower with the money intended for the bridge.

Dryslwyn Castle

A lovely spot, but not much left of the Castle. Café, toilets and picnic site.

24. A Connoisseur's Castle, a little town called Bethlehem, and the biggest Iron Age fort in Wales

Castell Carreg Cennen – Bethlehem – Y Garn Goch – Llandeilo and Dinefwr Park

Distance: 20mls/32km

Longer Option: From Bethlehem, if you continue to Llangadog and complete Ride 25, total will be 76mls/122km.

Shorter Option: Returning from Bethlehem without visiting Llandeilo would shorten ride to 16.5mls/26.5km

Terrain: Castle is built on top of a hill! Otherwise only moderate hills.

Accommodation/Refreshments/Supplies: Accommodation in Llandeilo as described in previous ride. Cafe at Castell Carreg Cennen. Cakes, Welsh cheeses for sale. Pub in Trapp. Supermarket/shops in Llandeilo. Cafe in Dinefwr Park.

Toilets: In car park at Castle. In Dinefwr Park.

Rail Access: Llandeilo.

Tourist Information: Shop at Castle, and in Llandeilo as described for previous ride.

Things to see on this Ride: Carreg Cennen Castle and Farm. Bethlehem Post Office. Iron Age Fort. Unspoilt hill country.

How to Connect with Next Ride: From Bethlehem to Llangadog is under 4mls/6.4km, where you can pick up route of Ride 25, Llandovery to Roman Gold Mines.

Route

Starting Point: The café in the farmyard at Castell Cerreg Cennen.

Those who wish can clamber up to the ramparts or take a tour while lazier companions stock up on calories before the ride. On offer is American coffee, Welsh cakes and bara brith (fruit bread), or at lunch,

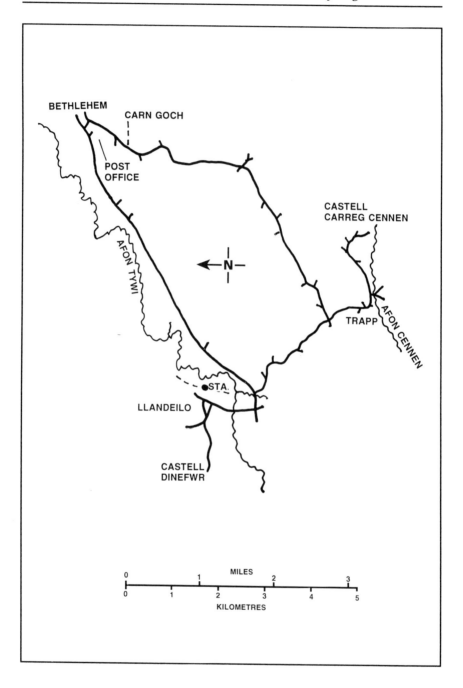

'cawl' (soup) with Welsh cheese. The tables in the farmyard are besieged by chickens, ducks, turkeys, sheep, dogs, little pink piglets and a peacock, all hoping for handouts.

When it's time to leave, exit through the car park and down the hill for a good whizz to start the day. In two minutes you're in Trapp, an attractive village with a jaunty air. Don't cross the river, but keep on up the hill, bearing slightly right. At the first crossroads, turn right for Bethlehem, riding uphill. At next crossroads, go straight over. The way to Bethlehem is as delightful and peaceful as its name suggests it ought to be. Short of the village, while still descending, turn right to view Y Garn Goch, one of the largest hill forts in Wales. Continue as you were, downhill, then climb into Bethlehem. At T-junction at top of rise, turn left, and 200 yards later, left again, signed to Ffairfach. The famous post office, much larger than the demands of a small village usually warrant, is a scene of great activity at Christmas. People travel long distances to have their mail specially franked here. (Connect from here to Llangadog for Ride 25 – see last paragraph of instructions, page 132.)

Within a couple of miles, as you breast a ridge, you'll see the silvery curves of the river Tywi immediately below you, and Llandeilo ahead on the opposite bank. The A40 can been seen in the distance, too far for its noise to disturb the tranquillity of the cattle in their water-bordered meadows.

In Ffairfach, keep straight ahead at junction, over small river Cennen and under railway bridge. Turn right at crossroads onto the A483 towards Llandeilo. (People riding from Gelli Aur, join here.) Cross river Tywi and climb beside a terrace of bright, colour-washed cottages. Turn left opposite the church as you enter One-Way system and left again as you leave it. Turn left at next junction signed to 'Free Car Park'. Just past the Police Station is the entrance to Dinefwr Park. The driveway is three quarters of a mile long and leads through the deer park.

Retrace steps to Ffairfach bridge and immediately turn right, by school, to return to Trapp and Castell Carreg Cennen, following the boundary of the Brecon Beacons National Park.

Castell Carreg Cennen

This is a Castle for anyone who ever revelled in romantic tales of Knights and maidens and battles long ago. 700 years old, it's a dramatic sight from every angle, perched on a crag of jagged rock 300ft/91m above the Tywi valley.

The farm has a flock of 'Balwen' Welsh Mountain Sheep. These are striking in appearance, having black or very dark brown bodies, but white faces, white socks, and tails.

Y Garn Goch

The fortifications, on a ridge 700ft above today's village, were the work of Iron Age tribes, made many centuries before the Romans came to Britain. From the top, "crowned with a stone cairn possibly 4000 years old", you have a commanding view of the Tywi valley.

Dinefwr Park

Leads to Newton House Mansion, dating from 1660. White Park Cattle are found here which derive from animals of a type known in the 10th century. Ruins of a mediaeval castle can be seen, but there's no access at the moment, because 'they're doing it up'.

25. 'There's Gold in them thar Hills'

Llandovery – Dolaucothi Roman Gold Mines – Talley Abbey – Llandovery

Distance: 34mls/55km.

Longer Option: From Llangadog take the A4069 south to Pont Newydd. Turn left for Talsarn or continue up Black Mountain past second hairpin for breath-taking views. Returning to Pont Newydd, turn right. Left in Talsarn for Myddfai. In under 3 miles keep left for Llandovery – an extra 14mls/23km or 22mls/35km.

Shorter Options: Returning from the Gold Mines on the A482, (normally a quiet road), will save several miles and avoid the more precipitous hills.

Terrain: Hilly to very hilly.

Accommodation/Refreshments/Supplies: Hotels and a good selection of B&Bs in Llandovery. Camping at Llangadog, Talsarn (book at Cross Inn), and at Brunant Arms, Caio. (ask in pub). B and B at Brunant Arms. Youth Hostel at Llanddeusant, 13mls/21km. Hostel accommodation for groups up to 14 in number at Dolaucothi Basecamp, Pumsaint, Llanwrda. Tel. 05585 359.

Self-catering cottages often available in the area. Pubs in Caio, Cilycwm, Crugybar, Talley, Llansadwrn. Umpteen pubs in Llangadog and Llandovery. Cafes at Gold mines and Felin Newydd. Good choice of small shops in Llandovery.

Toilets: Only if you go down the Mine first!

Rail Access: Llandovery.

Tourist Information: 8 Broad Street, Llandovery. Easter to September. Tel. 0550 20693

Things to see on this Ride: Hills and rivers. Real Ale Pub. Roman Gold Mine. Talley Abbey. Old Mill.

How to Connect with Next Ride: Leave Llandovery on the A4069, signed Llangadog. After 1.5 miles cross bridge and immediately turn left for Myddfai. In 1 mile, just over brow of hill, take unsigned left turning. Leave Myddfai towards Llanddeusant. At crossroads by Cross Inn turn left for Trecastle. Ride 3.5 miles. Enter Powys. After 2 miles cross stream by church at Pont Ar Hydfer. In half a mile turn right and climb 1.5 miles, through Glasfynydd Forest. Descend for 5 miles. Right on dual carriageway. One mile to Dan-yr-Ogoff.

Route

Starting Point: Market Square in Llandovery.

Exit town to north-west as if taking the A40 to Llandeilo. Go over level crossing and river Tywi, and immediately take first right into minor road. In one mile go right across river, and turn left at a T-junction. Follow beside river for 3mls/5km. Cross river by second bridge on left, signed Cilycwm. Turn right at the T-junction. At end of houses, turn left. Keep left when road makes two sharp corners where farm tracks join. Ride downhill, turn right at junction for Porthyrhyd. Climb past farm with ominous name of Pen y banc Isaf, (Lower Pen y banc). It takes much toil and sweat before you eventually pass the inevitable Pen y banc Uchaf (Higher Pen y banc).

The Post Office in Porthyrhyd is a counter installed in the living room of an ordinary house. At your knock, the Postperson cheerfully interrupts her housework to have a chat about the state of the world while she serves stamps, and emergency rations of sweets and chocolate. 'But I don't do any big shopping, mind'.

After Porthyrhyd take next right for Caio. From above, this little village looks very picturesque cuddled up beneath the hill, but you don't have much time to admire it – unless you'd like to climb back up! The Brunant Arms is an appealing pub with 15th century features and an interesting selection of beers. B & B available. The church opposite is Late Norman.

Take right fork on leaving Caio, up steep hill. Right at crossroads for Dolaucothi Gold Mines. Leaving the gold mines go straight ahead to the A482. Turn left and ride for 1.5 miles. At Bridgend Arms, route takes right fork onto the B4302, but a few yards ahead on the left hand side on the A482, is Felin Newydd watermill.

Go back to the B4302, continue through Crugbar, and on for 3.5mls/5.6km. After the turning from Llansawel has joined from your right, you pass a telephone on your left-hand side. In a few yards, take the unmarked turning to your right, beside a stone building. This becomes a delightful two mile ride around the lake. Excellent views of the Abbey and meadows across the water. After one mile, turn left past farm, at top of hill, to keep circling above the lake. A narrow, bumpy run down and you're beside the Abbey.

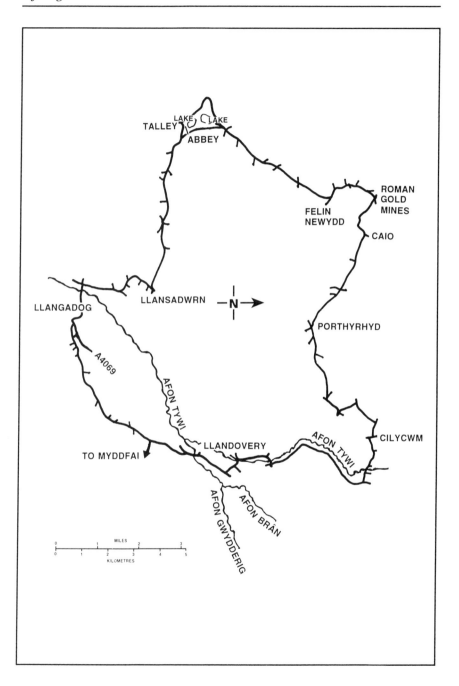

Leaving the Abbey, continue to village, with Post office on your left-hand side and Edwinsffordd Arms Hotel/Abbey Restaurant opposite. Turn right, signed Llandilo. Pass school and take left turn into small road which climbs steeply. The next bit was described to me in the pub – 'cross one mountain, wind a bit down, and go up like the side of a house over the next mountain'. Where there are four roads at a junction, take second from left into Llandsadwrn. From here you can look down on the river. Turn right, signed Llangadog, just before church. Turn right on joining the A40 and in a mile turn left to cross river Tywi and level crossing to reach Llangadog.

Go over a hump-backed bridge, up Church Street, past a wealth of pubs – the Red Lion, the Carpenters Arms, the Black Lion, all virtually next door to each other. Fork left at top of road by Black Lion, following signs to Llandovery. In a few yards turn right into Heol Pendref, a minor road, (signed Myddfai). Pass Recreation ground on your left and cemetery on your right. Keep straight on, an easy road. Over a stream on a sharp bend, then climb through woodland with a lovely run down the other side, to turn right and rejoin the A4069 one mile from Llandovery.

Roman Gold Mines

Try panning for gold, (finders keepers!). See the Romans' 2000-year old opencast workings, examine mine machinery, and finally go underground on a guided tour. Hard hats and safety lamps provided, but cycling shoes aren't the best footwear for scrambling over wet rocks.

The Dolaucothi Mines are administered by The National Trust. A café on the site serves both snacks and substantial meals. There is a well stocked shop, and toilets, but at the moment you must buy a ticket before you can make use of these facilities. Protests have been made and there may be a more sensible policy in future.

Talley Abbey

An artistic setting for a ruin, with green meadows sloping down to the lakes, under a rim of hills. The Abbey monks were not permitted to eat meat, but could enjoy fish. The Welsh name, Tal-y-llychau, means 'at the end of the lakes'. Alongside the Abbey is the Parish church. Bikes are not welcome in the churchyard, but if you park them at the top, a path leads through to the lake, a very pleasant spot for a picnic. An enclave in the Abbey grounds is dedicated to memorials of the Price family of Talley House. Daniel Price had six daughters, and David Long-Price had six sons. Their graves are annotated 'second daughter, third daughter' and so on. One hopes they had more individuality when alive.

Talley Abbey is open weekdays, 09.30 to 6.30, and Sundays 2 – 6.30. Tickets from cottage opposite. Toilets nearby.

Talley Abbey (Wales Tourist Board)

Felin Newydd

Tea rooms here with a good snack menu of home-baking, especially bara brith (a fruity tea-bread) and Welsh cakes. Shop sells the stone-ground wholemeal flour produced by the water mill. Geese and ducks of many kinds and colours live by the stream and are willing to be fed. Guided tours of mill between 10.30 and 5.30 pm. Toilets.

Llandovery/Llanymddyfri

Llandovery is a traditional market town, at the junction of ancient 'Drovers' Roads'. Livestock was driven from Pembrokeshire and Carmarthen all the way to Barnet Fair north of London. Geese had special bootees made for them to stop their webs getting sore on the march. Once an important staging post for coaches from London to Milford Haven, Llandovery is well supplied with places of refreshment. In the early 19th century there were 47 pubs and inns in the town. Their names give clues to their history. The Drovers' Arms is built over the old courtyard where the horses were brought in, and has a Jacobean door behind the bar. The King's Head Hotel relates to Charles the Second. This pub is on a corner, and has a 'preaching stone' from which people could be addressed in two directions at once.

Llandovery Castle was built around 1116 AD but was at the centre of many battles between Normans and Welsh and ruined during Owain Glyndŵr's rebellion in 1403.

Myddfai

Myddfai is an unspoilt village with a pleasant local pub, The Plough. An apt name for a predominantly agricultural community. In the 12th century, brothers known as 'The Physicians of Myddfai' were credited with magical healing powers. Their mother was said to be the mythical maiden of Llyn y Fan Fach, who rose from the lake to wed a farmer, but returned below the surface when he struck her for the third time.

26. Dinosaurs, Caves, a Singing Star and a Tall Fall

Henrhyden Falls – Craig-y-Nos – Dan-yr-Ogoff – Henrhyden

Distance: 11mls/18km. This ride is short because anyone wishing to visit the attractions may not have time for a long ride. Both Dan-yr-Ogoff and Craig-y-Nos are very popular and tend to be crowded in summer.

Longer Option: Keen cyclists won't be able to resist the mountains. Even if you rode here from Trecastle, riding the opposite way gives a different perspective. From Dan-yr-ogoff take the A4067 in the direction of Brecon, turning left just after beginning of dual carriageway to climb Bwlch Cerrig Duon (The Stony Pass) to Trecastle. Turn right on the A40 for 1.5 miles and right again for Crai. Turn right on the A4067 to return to Dan-yr-Ogof. 22mls/35.4km.

Terrain: Easy for the main ride, except for the twist in the tail. For the longer ride – you didn't want an easy life, did you?

Accommodation/Refreshments/Supplies: Accommodation is scarce in this area. Cave complex has Motel and Restaurant, open Easter to end of October. (Castle Hotel, 10 rooms, in Trecastle). Tea shop below Falls. Restaurant and Tea Rooms in Coach House, Craig-y-Nos, and Bar. Shop has confectionery. Pubs in Trecastle, if you go that way.

Toilets: Craig-y-Nos.

Rail Access: Neath. 16mls/25.7km.

Tourist Information: At Craig-y-Nos and Dan-yr-Ogof

Things to see on this Ride: The highest waterfall in Wales. Open Cast Mining. Craig-y-Nos, Home of Patti. Dan-yr-Ogof Showcaves and Dinosaur Park.

How to Connect with Next Ride: Ride north-east from Dan-yr-Ogoff on the A4067 for nearly 5mls/8km. Soon after you see the Cray reservoir on your left, take minor turning to right, signed Heol Senni. Ride for 3 miles 'up and over'. As you come down into Heol Senni, slow down, as you have to turn right before the bridge. Ride down for 1.5 miles and curve left to cross river. Turn right at junction to join Ride 27.

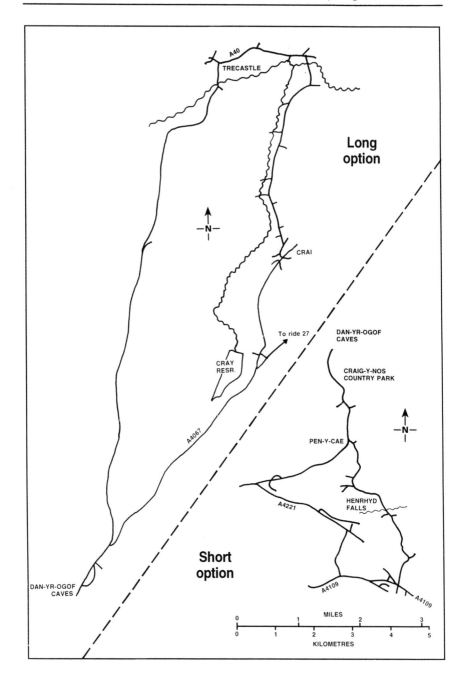

Route

Starting Point: Car Park at Henrhyd Falls.

From the Falls go down the hill and across river. Straight on uphill, signed Banwen. Banwen isn't actually on our route. It's not on anybody's route any more, though it occupies a once strategic position, on a Roman road leading to a Roman fort. The fort is now barely discernible, a grassy mound at the edge of a field. As often happens, the connection is kept alive by a name, and the road into Banwen is labelled 'Roman Road'.

At the crossroads with A4109 go right, then straightaway fork left at triangle, signed Dyffryn Cellwen. Just beyond Onllyn post office, turn right through an area of open cast mining – a weird environment of coal heaps and the tracks of monster lorries.

At a crossroads (slightly offset) with the A4221, go straight across and then turn left uphill at T-junction. This road runs parallel to the main road for a mile or so before rejoining it with a sharp bend. Go right on main road and near bottom of hill take acute-angled right turn onto the A4067 for 3mls/5km ride to Pen-y-cae. Craig y Nos is 1.5mls/2.5km straight ahead and Dan yr Ogoff 1.75mls/3km.

Return to Pen-y-cae and turn left in village, signed to Henrhyd Falls. The road is uphill, the only 'real' hill on the ride. Go for one mile, turn left at junction and continue climbing for another half mile. Falls are on your right as you begin to descend.

Henrhyd Falls

The Henrhyd (Old Ford) Falls on the Nant Llech (Slate Valley) river are the highest in South Wales, crashing 90ft/27.3m in a single bound. They are half a mile from the road. It's possible to walk 'to the end of the rainbow' behind the falls with their splintered sunbeams.

Craig-y-Nos (Rock of the Night)

A 40-acre park, once home of opera singer Adelina Patti. Visitor centre and countryside shop. Picnic facilities, but bikes are not allowed to be ridden in the grounds. Open daily all year except Christmas Day, from 10 am. The Coach House, outside the grounds, has a craft shop, licensed restaurant and tearooms in converted stables. Tel: 0639 730395

Dan-yr-Ogof (Under the Cave)

The caves were inhabited by prehistoric man and are the largest show-cave complex in Western Europe. Museum and Audio Visual Theatre. Craft Shop and Information centre. Restaurant and covered picnic area. Dinosaur Park. Open 7 days a week from April 1st, or Easter, to 31st October. Some facilities open in winter. Tel: 0693 730284. Winner of nine major tourism awards.

27. The Beacons Beckon!
A ride amid the peaks.

Brecon – Ystradfellte – Brecon

Distance: 37mls/59.5km

Shorter Option: Not including Brecon would reduce ride by 6.5mls/10.5km, but they're the easiest miles.

Terrain: One of the harder rides, but anyone who appreciates mountains will love it. The 11 year old daughter of friends of mine managed it very well with the help of plenty of Kit-Kat.

Accommodation/Refreshments/Supplies: Hotels in Brecon, some B and B's and self catering cottages and caravans. Youth Hostels: Llwyn-y-Celyn at Libanus, Brecon; Ty'n-y-Caeau at Groesffordd near Brecon and at Ystradfellte. Good selection of pubs, cafés and shops in Brecon. Stock up with portable goodies, and take lots of water.

Toilets: Storey Arms. Brecon. Mountain Centre. Ystradfellte.

Rail Access: Nearest stations Abergavenny, 17mls/27km or Merthyr Tydfil 18mls/29km.

Tourist Information: In Brecon. At Mountain Centre.

Things to see on this Ride: The Brecon Beacons, mountain scenery, waterfalls. Subterranean Rivers and Caves at Ystradfellte.

How to Connect with Next Ride: At junction with the A4059, turn right for Penderyn, and continue to Hirwaun. In Hirwaun, turn right at junction where sign says innocently 'A4061. Treherbert 8.' It doesn't lie – 8 miles it is, but don't think in terms of a brisk half-hour run. Go straight on at first roundabout (second exit) and left at next roundabout. Pass the Tower colliery and begin a massive climb. A superb introduction to the Rhondda. After 4.5 miles, punctuated by stops to admire the views, there is a 'Welcome to Rhondda' sign and you start down into the valley. Ride straight through a string of towns with traditional stone terraced homes and neighbourhood shops – Treherbert, Treorchi, Pentre, Ystrad, Llwynypia, Trealaw and Porth. In Porth turn right at roundabout, follow signs to Pontypridd. 22mls/35.4km.

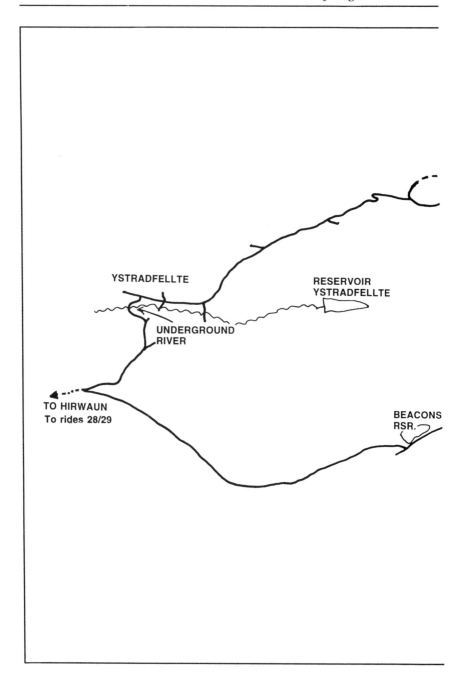

YSTRADFELLTE

RESERVOIR
YSTRADFELLTE

UNDERGROUND
RIVER

TO HIRWAUN
To rides 28/29

BEACONS
RSR.

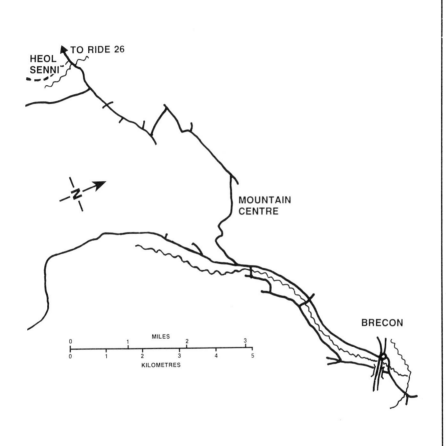

HEOL SENNI

TO RIDE 26

MOUNTAIN CENTRE

BRECON

MILES
0   1   2   3
0   1   2   3   4   5
KILOMETRES

Route

Starting Point: Parking area on the A470, half a mile south of Storey Arms Outdoor Centre.

Walkers and climbers congregate here before setting off to conquer Pen y Fan, the highest peak of the Brecon Beacons. In summer there's a kiosk for tea, hot dogs and ices. Toilets.

Pen y Fan (2880ft/886m) with its distinctive overhang, and Corn Du (2837ft/873m) are directly above to your right. Turn right towards Brecon for a good start to the day – 8mls/13km of smooth descent – time to sit back and enjoy the lush hillsides and the waterfalls tumbling right to your feet. The road along the other side of the gully is a 'Green' road, traditionally used by drovers. Pass the Llwyn-y-Celyn Youth Hostel on your right and the turning to Libanus Mountain Centre on your left. Enter Brecon from roundabout where the A470 joins the A40.

On leaving Brecon, turn left into Ffrwdgrech road, opposite The Drovers pub, before reaching the roundabout. Road goes under the A40. In one mile, at junction, take furthest right of three roads. Signs prohibit entry of military vehicles to this road and the middle one. After one mile, Gilwhybert Motte, an impressively massive mound surrounded by a ditch, is close by the road on your left. Go ahead at junction as road narrows. Take next turning to right, downhill. Ride beside small stream. Wildlife is prolific here. You may disturb a heron, a water rat or a shrew, as well as squirrels and rabbits.

In summer, the trees and hedgerows are over-luxuriant and hamper your view of the water. Cross the stream by Libanus Mill Farm and the old mill house Felin Fach. Regain the A470. Turn left, uphill, and take first turning right, signed National Park Visitors' Centre. Watch out for cattle grid at entrance to Mountain Centre. On from the Mountain Centre, continue onto open moorland, and ride for 1.5 miles. Several more cattle grids. Turn left over stream with flood level marked up to 9ft/2.7m. Go left on joining main road, and in half a mile turn right at junction signed Heol Senni/Ystradfellte.

Savour the hill, but watch for turning signed to Ystradfellte on your left – easy to overshoot it!

Keep left at junction, again signed to Ystradfellte, 9 miles. (People continuing from Ride 26 join here from the right).

Now you must pay for your fun. The next section is a hard pull, with a couple of savage hairpins dragging you up 1500ft/448m in three-quarters of a mile. The mountains crowd around you, presenting magnificent views of the surrounding peaks and the Senni valley.

Run down the other side, keeping straight ahead into Ystradfellte. There are gates across the road. A local farmer claims to have had 'hundreds' of sheep lost or stolen. In Ystradfellte, turn right by the New Inn, but not into dead-end road. (The church is on your left, and should you need them, the Post Office, ' open mornings and as announced', and Toilets are a bit further on past the church).

After half a mile, turn left into very narrow lane which makes an off-set crossroads with a gated farm track. Ride downhill for another half a mile, to a car park on your left at Porth yr Ogof (Gateway to the Cave). From here you can have a quick scramble down the bank to see the river Mellte swirling on its boulder-strewn way and disappearing into the cavern. It runs underground for 250 yards/228m. If you have time and inclination for a bit of walking, it's easy to follow the way-marking to see the resurgence at the Blue Pool. (About 20 minutes for the return trip). There are a number of waterfalls further on. On a warm day, the water can look enticing, but it's dangerously cold. Once in early spring I was tempted to have a dip. I discovered why it's called 'The Blue Pool' – I was blue for hours! Paths are rough going and slippery, so take care. Toilets in car park and an Information board.

Continue the way you were going, up a stiff hill, and in half a mile turn right. Keep right, signed Penderyn/Brecon after another half mile. Turn left onto the A4059, northwards, towards Brecon. (Turn right here to join Rides 28/29).

This is classified as an 'A' road, but it's a wide comfortable road without heavy traffic. There are excellent views of the Beacons, and although it's a steady uphill gradient it's not hard. Turn left onto the A470 when latter joins from the right at bottom of hill, by corner of Beacons Reservoir. Ride beside reservoir for half a mile back to starting point.

Brecon/Aberhonddu

Ringed by the mountains, at the confluence of the rivers Usk and Honddu, Brecon is on the edge of the Brecon Beacons National Park, and is orientated towards the outdoors.

The Castle of Brecon Hotel's grounds are the place to see what remains of the Norman castle. St John's church was upgraded to Cathedral status in 1923. It's large for a church but lacks the splendour of longer established Cathedrals, though it has 13th and 14th century features. Brecon also has a Museum and a boys' public school, Christ's Hospital, founded by Royal Charter in 1541.

The Castle of Brecon Hotel, set into the remains of the castle

Storey Arms

Outdoor Education Centre and Mountain Rescue Post.

Mountain Centre:

Café with large outdoor terrace overlooking mountains, and indoor seating. Toilets. Information. Shop for books, maps and souvenirs. Open all year except Christmas Day. Tel: 0874 623366.

Ystradfellte

Known as 'The Waterfall Country', and famous with cavers and potholers.

28. Minting Money

Pontypridd to Llantrisant: home of the Royal Mint

Distance: 21.5mls/34.5km.

Longer Option: This ride and the next can both be enjoyed in the same day by go-for-it cyclists.

Shorter Option: Using the Taff trail to return to Pontypridd saves the 1.5 miles up the mountain.

Terrain: Only a couple of hills, but biggies – 1181ft/360m in 1.5 miles, up to Eglwysilan.

Accommodation/Refreshments/Supplies. See next ride for accommodation details. Pubs and basic shops in Llantrisant. Hot drinks at Model House. Pubs, cafés, shops in Pontypridd, and pubs en route – The Ship near Efail Isaf. Upper Boat pub. Rose and Crown at Eglwysilan, (a good reason for going that way). Post Office/Shops in Beddau.

Toilets: In Llantrisant at the Model House, and on way out of town. In Pontypridd at Bus Station and in Sardis Road.

Rail Access: Pontypridd.

Tourist Information: In Pontypridd, near the Old Bridge.

Things to see on this Ride: Llantrisant. The Model House Exhibition and Craft Centre. The Royal Mint. Farms and surprisingly rural views close to an industrial area. Pontypridd described in following Ride.

How to Connect with Next Ride: Next ride begins in Pontypridd.

Route

Starting Point: Pontypridd Railway Station.

Face the station and take the road immediately to the left, which goes under the railway track. (Llantrisant Road). Climb for two miles, reaching 720ft/220m.

After an uneventful couple of miles, go straight across roundabout at Beddau and continue sedate descent into Llantrisant. At the traffic lights with Cross Keys on the corner, turn right up steep rise into the Bull Ring central square, with statue of the self-styled Arch-Druid of Wales, Dr. Price. The Model House is worth a visit.

Leave the square by the main (uncobbled) road, Heol y Sarn, with the Bear on your right and statue to your left. Down a steep hill, over a cattle grid. There are loose horses and ponies on the common. Turn left after the cattle grid at the end of the road. The Royal Mint is on your right after half a mile. Retrace steps as far as Beddau.

Turn right at roundabout into Gwaun Miskin Road and ride downhill through housing area. Keep straight on for one mile. At off-set cross-

A rural lane near Pontypridd. High hedges reduce visibility.

roads with the A473, go across, right-left, signed Efail Isaf, then under the bridge and turn left. Cross small river. At junction turn right in front of The Ship, cross bridge and immediately go left, signed Efail Isaf. Ride through village and turn left by the Carpenters Arms, into Fford y Capel road, signed Church Village. Turn right at the Chapel into narrow road.

Ride for one mile, and turn left. It's difficult to identify this turning, but it's the first one you come to, apart from farm entrances. A downhill run for a mile, to a junction with a grassy triangle in the middle. Keep left, on the level at first, then down. At bottom of hill go right into even smaller road past farm. At junction with main road, go

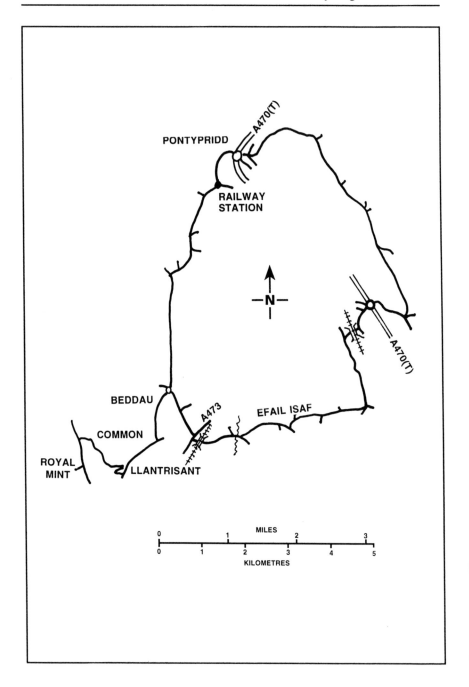

right, under railway bridge. Shortly, go left across river, with Upper Boat pub to your left.

Join roundabout and take exit after passing underneath the A470, signed Eglwysilan. Turn right, uphill. At the bridge on the bend, you can get down to the Taff Trail on the right-hand side, if you wish. It's 3.5 miles back to Pontypridd from here.

Those who don't mind a climb will find it worthwhile to turn left up the hill to Eglwysilan. It's steep for half a mile, then less so for a mile. The Rose and Crown and the church appear suddenly on your left, on a little plateau. You're not at the top yet, but both merit a visit. Go left at crossroads and climb out onto open moorland. The views of the built-up valley make a tremendous contrast with the emptiness of the hilltop.

As you start down, there's a cattle grid to cross before you let rip. It's two miles of bliss through woods with a little stream dodging from side to side. Pass Pontypridd Golf Club and the road to the Cottage Hospital. At crossroads with main road, go straight over, still downhill, to the town centre in Pontypridd.

Llantrisant

Dedicated to a threesome of Saints, Llantrisant is built on a hill, dominated by its church. Originally Norman, it was first restored in Tudor times and then rebuilt in the by the Victorians. There's little left of the nearby Castle now, though its situation, dominating the Vale of Glamorgan, gave it great importance around 1250 AD. There were fashions in castle building and this was the 'golden age.' Innovations from France such as arrow slits and round rather than oblong towers were the latest state of the art. Round towers were such a desired feature that castles which didn't have them, added them on, as at Usk.

Dr. Price, whose statue is in the Bull Ring, must have been a colourful character to say the least. He's shown with flowing hair and cloak, with theatrically outstretched arms. His conviction that cremation ought to be legalised led him to burn the body of his infant son on Llantrisant common, which caused outrage in 1884.

The Model House Craft and Design Centre in the Bull Ring has studios where the public may watch people working in many different crafts. As well, there's an Exhibition on the history and making of coins and the work of the Royal Mint. Shop, toilets, hot drinks. (More café facilities planned). Open 10 – 5 Tuesday to Sunday. Closed Mondays.

The Royal Mint

Here you can buy gold and silver coins from around the world, – coins like a $100 silver coin from The Cook Islands, a New Zealand Coronation Anniversary Crown piece, and gold sovereigns, as well as special sets of coins for Weddings and new babies. Prices range from under £10 to four figures. You can also join the Royal Mint Coin Club. Call at the Main Entrance between 9am – 4pm Monday to Friday. A receptionist will take your name and arrange for your purchases to be brought to you. Enquiries on 0443 223880. Groups of more than 3 or 4 people should telephone in advance of their intended visit.

29. Black Gold

A Tour of the Rhondda Valleys

Distance: 19mls/30.5km

Options: No shorter but avoids one stiff hill if you take the road up the Rhondda Fach from Porth.

Terrain: Only a couple of hills! (The Welsh like to think they're mountains).

Accommodation/Refreshments/Supplies: Hotel at Rhondda Heritage Centre. Youth Hostel at Glyncornel Centre, Llwynypia, Rhondda. Pontypridd has many cafés/shops. Coffee shop at Rhondda Heritage Park. Pub at Llanwonno.

Toilets: By Bus Station and in Sardis Road.

Rail Access: Pontypridd.

Tourist Information: At Heritage Centre. In Pontypridd, near the Old Bridge. Tel: 0443 402077.

Things to see on this Ride: Rhondda Valleys – everyone's image of Wales. Rhondda Heritage Park. St Gwonno's church. Mountain scenery. Those who climb an extra hill will also visit the Shrine of St Mary of Penrhys.

Connections: This ride ends the South Wales tour. To return to Cardiff, use the Taff Trail, a path prepared for cyclists and walkers along disused tram and railways, or canal and river banks. It links Cardiff to Brecon in three stages, Cardiff to Pontypridd, Pontypridd to Merthyr Tydfil, and Merthyr Tydfil to Talybont-on-Usk. Leaflets with maps which describe each section in detail are available from Tourist Information Centres.

Route

Starting Point: Pontypridd Railway Station.

Turn left and take the A4058 signed to Rhondda Valleys. Ride with the river on your left, through Hopkinstown, for a couple of flat miles. Entering Trehafod, take left turning, ride through village, past back of station. Rhondda Heritage Park on your right. Leave the Heritage Centre and rejoin main road. Keep left at roundabout. (Don't cross river).

(If you're taking the easier option, go straight through Porth, bear right at roundabout onto the A4233 for Ferndale, passing through Ynyshir, Wattstown, Pontygwaith and Tylorstown, where the other route rejoins).

For the longer ride:

In centre of Porth, at complicated junction, keep left to cross river and immediately turn right. Signs are for Tonypandy and Dinas. (Effectively you have kept to the same road, but it's now the B4278). More flat riding along valley. Royal Worcester Factory Shop on your right.

By Tonypandy railway station, turn right at roundabout, over river and left onto the A4058. Ride through Trealaw and Llwynypia, and carry on to Ystrad. In Ystrad turn right between Star Hotel and church, just before traffic lights, signed Tylorstown. A mile-long hill up. Roundabout just as you pull yourself over the summit. Shrine to Our Lady of Penrhys on your right, commanding view of both Rhondda valleys.

Back round the roundabout, take Ferndale exit, enjoy descent for 1.5 miles. Left at bottom, the A4233, signed to Ferndale. Climb through Tylorstown and on into Ferndale.

At end of street, start down, but turn right again on next bend by Anchor pub, signed to Llanwonno. This is a ticklish double bend, go carefully. Rapid descent towards river, and across bridge into Blaenllechau. You're into the hardest but last hill of the day – two miles and steep with it. At the top of first stretch, there's an acute right turn – you need speed and a clear road or you won't manage it. Don't tangle with cars here, their problems are worse than yours. To avoid getting off, ride ahead and turn on the level, to approach from the opposite direction. The mountain road is narrow but the surface is excellent. Views all the way up make walking a pleasure! In spring there are wild flowers, in late summer the hills are purple with heather and in autumn the woods are fiery with reds and golds. Rows of terraced houses, all with slate roofs but painted in various colours, and the thread of the river below, make a backdrop any film director would weep for. From the summit (1300ft/400m) you can see Tylorstown Tip, a greened-over mound of colliery spoil, known as 'Old Smoky'. Large scale Bronze Age burial sites have been found on Llanwonno ridge.

Down into the cool of the Forestry road for a mile, to reach St Gwonno's church and Brynffynon pub. When it's time to go, either of

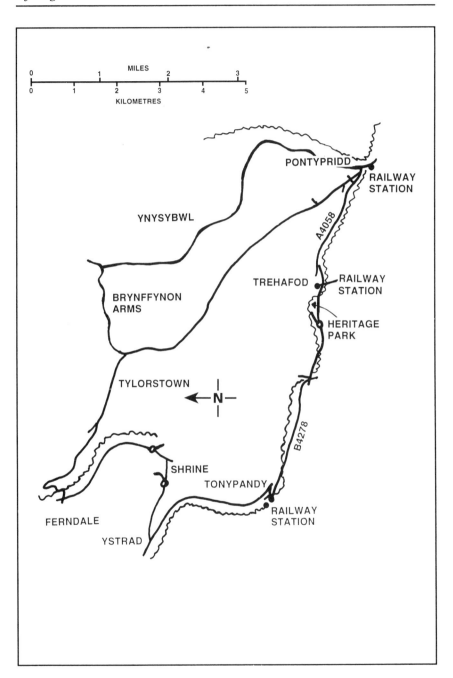

the roads from the pub will take you to Pontypridd. It's six miles and down hill all the way.

The road below the pub takes a lively dive through the woods. Right at a T-junction, down to Ynysbwl, follow the stream to the Old Bridge in Pontypridd. The road behind the pub offers a quieter route. A gentler descent through more open country (much tree-felling here). It steepens for last half-mile into Pontypridd.

Pontypridd

The Taff and the Rhondda Valleys join here. The 'Old Bridge' built in 1755, was once the largest single-arch bridge in the world. Still pictures-que, it's now demoted to a footbridge.

Rhondda Heritage Park

Based in the restored buildings of the Lewis Merthyr Colliery, which closed in 1983. Guided Tours led by former miners. Audio-visual presen-tation of the story of coal mining from the viewpoint of a mining family covering three generations. Shop, Cafe, Children's Play Park. Hotel adjoining.

St Gwonno's Church

The key to the church is kept behind the bar of the Brynffynon Arms. St Gwonno was one of the early monks who brought Christianity to Wales. The graveyard runs away down the incline and is surprisingly roomy considering that the only other building within miles is the pub! Many of the inscriptions are in Welsh, but the memorial to Guto Nyth Bran (Griffith Morgan) is in English. He's noted for running 12 miles (19km) in 53 minutes, but he died at age 37 so it wasn't much good as a keep-fit exercise.

The Shrine of Our Lady at Penrhys

This was a place of pilgrimage for many hundreds of years. The Statue commands a view over the Rhondda from the site of a Grange built by Cistercian Monks in the early 1300s. The now grassy coal tips and wooded slopes of the valley make it possible to imagine the pre-industrial scene. Older inhabitants remember being brought to drink the waters of a Holy Well here, before World War 2, but there seems to be no trace of it now.

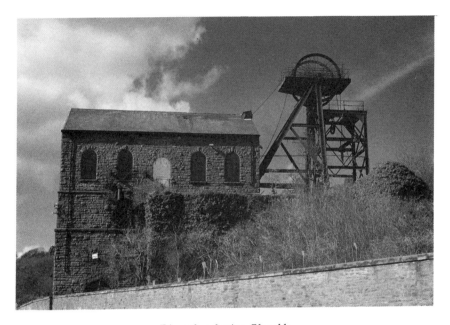

Disused coal mine, Rhondda

Appendix

Where to Stay

Basic accommodation for groups can sometimes be arranged in Leisure Centres, or Community Halls. Contact the Town Clerk or the County Council Leisure Services Department of the district concerned.

Yellow Pages have lists of Hotels and Guest Houses. You can see the Directories for most areas of Wales in Public Libraries and Main Post Offices.

If your home town happens to be 'twinned' with a place you want to visit in Wales, you're in luck! Town twinning committees are very helpful.

Youth Hostels offer budget price accommodation. Family rooms for parents with children under 5 at some hostels. Out of season, some entire hostels may be rented. Groups of 5 or more qualify for a membership concession. Book-a-Bed system (not all hostels). Self catering, or many hostels provide breakfast, evening meal and lunch packs. Join at any staffed hostel, or contact

Youth Hostels Association (Head Office), Trevelyan House, 8 St Stephen's Hill, St Albans, Herts AL1 2DY. Tel: 0727 55215

Tourist Information Centres in South Wales

TICs operate a free Bed Booking service and are useful sources of information on current local events. Some are open April to September only. The following TICs are open all year.

Wales Tourist Board: Dept RJ1, PO Box 1, Cardiff CF1 1XN. Tel: 0222 227281

Brecon: Cattle Market Car Park, Brecon, Powys LD3 9DA. Tel: 0874 622485

Caerleon: Ffwrrwm Art and Craft Centre, High Street, Caerleon, Gwent NP6 1AG. Tel: 0633 430777

Cardiff: Cardiff Marketing, Cardiff Central Railway Station. Tel: 0222 227281.

Carmarthen: Lammas Street, Carmarthen SA31 3AQ. Tel: 0267 231557

Fishguard: 4 Hamilton Street, Fishguard SA65 9HL. Tel: 0348 873484

Newport: Newport Museum and Art Gallery, John Frost Square, Gwent NP9 1HZ. Tel: 0633 842962

Swansea: PO Box 59, Singleton Street, Swansea SA1 3QN. Tel: 0792 468321

Tenby: The Croft, Tenby SA70 8AP. 0834 842402

Information for Cyclists

The CTC (Cyclists' Touring Club) is Britain's largest national cycling organisation. They provide technical advice, legal aid and insurance for members. They also produce a Cycle Hire Directory, listing cycle hire centres throughout the U.K. where you may hire every type of bicycle, and also extras such as child seats and panniers. Subscription £15 per annum.

Cyclists' Touring Club, 69, Meadrow, Godalming, Surrey GU7 3HS. Tel: 0483 417217